PRENTICE HALL *WRITER'S SOLUTION*

Grammar Practice Book

PLATINUM

PRENTICE HALL
Upper Saddle River, New Jersey
Needham, Massachusetts

ISBN 0-13-434643-2

5 6 7 8 9 10   01 00

PRENTICE HALL
Simon & Schuster Education Group
A VIACOM COMPANY

Contents

1.1 Nouns

Nouns as Names

A noun is the name of a person, place, or thing. Nouns that name things that can be seen, touched, or recognized through any of the five senses are called concrete nouns. Nouns that name things that can not be recognized through any of the five senses are called abstract nouns.

Concrete Nouns		Abstract Nouns	
beach	tree	dismay	happiness
moose	Judy	wisdom	courage
hotel	sand	treatment	honor
Europe	table	decision	oppression

Compound Nouns

A compound noun is a noun that is made up of more than one word.

TYPES OF COMPOUND NOUNS		
Separate Words	Hyphenated Words	Combined Words
soap opera	jack-of-all-trades	dishwasher
fire engine	commander-in-chief	toothbrush

EXERCISE A: Identifying Nouns. Underline each concrete noun. Circle each abstract noun. The number in parentheses tells how many nouns there are.

EXAMPLE: Erica has high (hopes) for her (future.) (3)

1. The Constitution guarantees many different rights. (2)
2. The biggest concern of the hikers was time. (3)
3. The grace of the long-legged birds surprised the tourists. (3)
4. Paula overcame her fear of success. (3)
5. The difference between Lou and Len is their attitude. (4)
6. Several hunters came back with deer, elk, and moose. (4)
7. Has the doctor given Sherry any good advice? (3)
8. An article in the newspaper describes the opening of Marvelle Park. (4)
9. A sign outside the auditorium listed the soloists. (3)
10. A nurse at the hospital put a splint on my arm. (4)

EXERCISE B: Recognizing Compound Nouns. Circle each compound noun. Underline all other nouns.

EXAMPLE: Andrew's favorite <u>thing</u> at the (playground) is the (seesaw.)

1. The scientist had a breakthrough in her research.
2. The birdwatcher made his way through the underbrush.
3. That player hit two home runs in the same game.
4. The host was unable to seat all the guests in the dining room.
5. My stepmother is recovering well from her heart attack.
6. A jack-in-the-box is a perfect toy for a two-year-old.
7. The recent heat wave broke all previous records.
8. What are your plans after high school?
9. Spring-cleaning is a chore that few people like.
10. The actor stepped into the spotlight.

1.1 Nouns

Common and Proper Nouns

A common noun names any one of a class of people, places, or things. A proper noun names a specific person, place, or thing. Each important word in a proper noun begins with a capital letter.

Common Nouns		Proper Nouns	
book	desert	Statue of Liberty	Asia
holiday	leader	Gettysburg Address	Texas
car	composer	*Jane Eyre*	Lassie
country	horse	Mercury	Canada

EXERCISE A: Recognizing Proper Nouns. Write the proper noun in each sentence in the blank at the right, adding the missing capitalization.

EXAMPLE: My favorite poet is emily dickinson.   *Emily Dickinson*

1. The brooklyn bridge has been featured in many movies. _____

2. Many famous prisoners have been held in the tower of london. _____

3. The bulldogs are the leading team in our league. _____

4. My cousin is a senior at jackson high school. _____

5. At this time of year, tomatoes come from california. _____

6. Have you been in the new shop on willow street? _____

7. This book is a biography of abigail adams. _____

8. I hope uncle mike will visit this weekend. _____

9. Do you know the capital of montana? _____

10. Whose faces appear on mount rushmore? _____

EXERCISE B: Adding Proper Nouns to Sentences. Fill in each blank with a proper noun.

EXAMPLE: I bought a new album by ___*Elton John*___.

1. Have you eaten at the new restaurant on _____?

2. At the end of the close game, the _____ were the winners.

3. Last summer we visited _____ on vacation.

4. The _____ is a famous landmark in our nation's capital.

5. Didn't you lend that book to _____?

6. The new bridge will cross the _____.

7. Our next-door neighbors are moving to _____.

8. The chef has opened a health-food restaurant called _____.

9. Our new car is a _____.

10. An author I admire is _____.

1.2 Pronouns

Antecedents of Pronouns

A pronoun is a word used to take the place of a noun or group of words acting as a noun. An antecedent is the noun (or group of words acting as a noun) for which a pronoun stands.

PRONOUNS AND ANTECEDENTS

ANTECEDENT   PRONOUN   PRONOUN
The [Hobsons] built *their* back porch *themselves*.

PRONOUN   ANTECEDENT
That is the [house] Jim hopes to buy.

ANTECEDENT   PRONOUN   ANTECEDENT   PRONOUN
[Jonathan,] pass me *some* of the [salad] Jane and *you* made.

EXERCISE A: Identifying Antecedents. Circle the antecedent of each underlined pronoun.

EXAMPLE: (Jill) will let you have <u>some</u> of the (milkshake) if you ask <u>her</u>.

1. Without <u>his</u> parents' permission, Al could not go on the field trip.
2. <u>Most</u> of the critics liked the play.
3. The man <u>who</u> greeted Sally at the door asked to see <u>her</u> ticket.
4. Hannah, have <u>you</u> decided <u>which</u> of the bikes to buy?
5. Climbing to the top of the Washington Monument was fun, but <u>it</u> tired us.
6. The huge old trunk was <u>something</u> the bride and groom never expected.
7. <u>Several</u> of the students completed <u>their</u> papers early.
8. <u>Which</u> of the twins was <u>that</u>?
9. Anthony quickly told Mrs. Lee how much <u>he</u> appreciated <u>her</u> kindness.
10. The senator <u>who</u> introduced the bill worked hard for <u>its</u> passage.

EXERCISE B: Adding Pronouns to Match Antecedents. Find the antecedent for a pronoun that could fill in each blank. Then write the appropriate pronoun for that antecedent.

EXAMPLE: The Hornets owe much of ___*their*___ success to Coach Maloney.

1. Paul went to school without _____ lunch money.
2. To find the area of a rectangle, multiply _____ length by _____ width.
3. Jenny, would _____ like _____ of this cake?
4. Although the leaves are changing later this year, _____ colors are more vivid than usual.
5. Without _____ help, Pete, we would still be working.
6. Mayor Anita Rimirez announced _____ plans to seek a second term.
7. The woman _____ once baby-sat for my brother still sends _____ a Christmas card every year.
8. Two robins made _____ nest in the maple tree.
9. One explanation for the show's success is _____ appeal to teenagers.
10. If _____ of the players show confidence, the other players are likely to follow _____ example.

1.2 Pronouns

Personal, Reflexive, and Intensive Pronouns

Personal pronouns refer to the person speaking, the person spoken to, or the person, place, or thing spoken about. A reflexive pronoun ends in -*self* or -*selves* and adds information to a sentence by pointing back to a noun or pronoun earlier in the sentence. An intensive pronoun ends in -*self* or -*selves* and simply adds emphasis to a noun or pronoun in the same sentence.

Personal Pronouns		Reflexive and Intensive Pronouns	
Singular	**Plural**	**Singular**	**Plural**
I, me, my, mine	we, us, our, ours	myself	ourselves
you, your, yours	you, your, yours	yourself	yourselves
he, him, his, she,	they, them, their,	himself, herself,	themselves
her, hers, it, its	theirs	itself	

EXAMPLES: *She* and *I* will help *you* with that job.   (personal pronouns)
Tom fixed *himself* a bedtime snack.   (reflexive pronoun)
Mom fixed the car *herself*.   (intensive pronoun)

EXERCISE A: Identifying Personal, Reflexive, and Intensive Pronouns. Underline the pronoun in each sentence. In the blank, write whether it is *personal, intensive,* or *reflexive*.

EXAMPLE: Pam and I enjoyed the concert. _____*personal*_____

1. The tourists suddenly found themselves in a strange part of town. _____

2. The loud music from next door interrupted my studying. _____

3. The neighbors cleaned up the block themselves. _____

4. Mom, prepare yourself for some exciting news. _____

5. The star made his way through the crowd of screaming fans. _____

6. Jillian packed the footlocker herself. _____

7. The salad dressing has too much vinegar in it. _____

8. The President himself will greet the Prime Minister. _____

9. The children amused themselves by playing checkers. _____

10. Please complete your assignment by Friday. _____

EXERCISE B: Adding Personal, Reflexive, and Intensive Pronouns to Sentences. Fill in each blank with an appropriate pronoun of the kind called for in parentheses.

EXAMPLE: Ladies and gentlemen, please help _____*yourselves*_____ .   (reflexive)

1. Do all these candies have coconut inside _____ ?   (personal)

2. We told _____ that we were imagining things.   (reflexive)

3. The news show has changed _____ format this season.   (personal)

4. I _____ favor a dress code.   (intensive)

5. After the first few seconds, Kathy regained _____ confidence.   (personal)

6. In spite of all _____ studying, Ken was nervous about the test.   (personal)

7. We found _____ wondering what to do next.   (reflexive)

8. Mike and I gave _____ reports.   (personal)

9. The committee members decided among _____ on the date.   (reflexive)

10. The poet read her newest work _____ .   (intensive)

1.2 Pronouns

Demonstrative, Relative, and Interrogative Pronouns

Demonstrative pronouns direct attention to specific people, places, or things.

DEMONSTRATIVE PRONOUNS			
this	that	these	those

A relative pronoun begins a subordinate clause and connects it to another idea in the sentence.

RELATIVE PRONOUNS				
that	which	who	whom	whose

An interrogative pronoun is used to begin a question.

INTERROGATIVE PRONOUNS				
what	which	who	whom	whose

EXERCISE A: Recognizing Demonstrative, Relative, and Interrogative Pronouns. On the blank at the right, write whether each sentence contains a demonstrative, relative, or interrogative pronoun.

EXAMPLE: What shall we do? __*interrogative*__

1. That was a wonderful movie. _____

2. Here is a person whom I want you to meet. _____

3. Who told you the password? _____

4. The article, which was written by a senator, was interesting. _____

5. Which of the notebooks is yours? _____

6. These are excellent baked apples. _____

7. Whom did you meet at the library? _____

8. Do you know anyone who can help us? _____

9. This is the author's first book. _____

10. Where is the picture that you painted? _____

EXERCISE B: Adding Demonstrative, Relative, and Interrogative Pronouns to Sentences. Fill in each blank with an appropriate demonstrative, relative, or interrogative pronoun.

EXAMPLE: This package feels heavier than __*that*__.

1. _____ of the colors do you prefer?

2. Are _____ the right glasses?

3. The family from _____ we bought the house had owned it for years.

4. Alice made the decision _____ she thought was best.

5. _____ is bringing the salad?

6. _____ is slightly lighter than that.

7. _____ gave you the application forms?

8. Is there anyone _____ can advise you?

9. Behind _____ of the doors is the treasure chest?

10. _____ are you going to do next?

1.2 Pronouns

Indefinite Pronouns

Indefinite pronouns refer to people, places, or things, often without specifying which ones.

INDEFINITE PRONOUNS			
Singular		**Plural**	**Singular or Plural**
another	much	both	all
anybody	neither	few	any
anyone	nobody	many	more
anything	no one	others	most
each	nothing	several	none
either	one		some
everybody	other		
everyone	somebody		
everything	someone		
little	something		

EXERCISE A: Recognizing Indefinite Pronouns. Underline each indefinite pronoun in the sentences below.

EXAMPLE: If <u>neither</u> of these scarves is acceptable, I can show you <u>others</u>.

1. Everyone on the team had the same goals.
2. Someone has already eaten most of the cookies.
3. Each of the actors was nervous about dress rehearsal.
4. None of the guests had much to eat.
5. Few of the officials would admit that anything was wrong.
6. Does either of the candidates seem better than the other?
7. Both of the twins fool everyone by switching places.
8. Several of the speakers suggested that much remained to be done.
9. No one denied that something definite should be done.
10. Many of my classmates find fault with everything.

EXERCISE B: Adding Indefinite Pronouns to Sentences. Fill in each blank with an indefinite pronoun that makes sense.

EXAMPLE: Has ___*anyone*___ called for me?

1. _____ of my friends plan to go to college.
2. Is _____ of these the style you had in mind?
3. Mike's size is surprising, considering how _____ he eats.
4. The mayor said _____ about her future plans.
5. This book tells _____ you will ever need to know about seashells.
6. These boots are more expensive than _____ .
7. _____ about that house is very attractive.
8. Would you like to have _____ of this pie?
9. Tonight's paper says _____ about the election returns.
10. _____ in the new park is appealing to children.

1.3 Action Verbs and Linking Verbs

Action Verbs

A verb is a word that expresses time while showing an action, a condition, or the fact that something exists. An action verb is a verb that tells what action someone or something is performing.

Visible Action	Mental Action
Jeremy *ate* the whole pizza.	Elena *wondered* about her future.

Transitive and Intransitive Verbs

An action verb is transitive if it directs action toward someone or something named in the same sentence. An action verb is intransitive if it does not direct action toward someone or something named in the same sentence. The word that receives the action of a transitive verb is the object of the verb.

Transitive	Intransitive
The host *interviewed* Sue. (interviewed *whom*?) Sue	Sue *smiled* when she won. (smiled what?) no answer

EXERCISE A: Recognizing Action Verbs. Underline the action verb in each sentence. In the blank, write whether the action is *V* (visible) or *M* (mental).

EXAMPLE: Tristan <u>forgot</u> the assignment. __*M*__

1. Wendy thought about the puzzle for hours. _____
2. The auctioneer pointed toward the woman in the back row. _____
3. The pendulum of the grandfather's clock swung rhythmically. _____
4. Dana decided early on the topic for her essay. _____
5. The committee made posters to announce the next dance. _____
6. Betsy plays golf every weekend. _____
7. The tennis players sipped lemonade between sets. _____
8. Both the politicians considered withdrawing from the campaign. _____
9. Tracy drew up a plan for us to follow. _____
10. The star entered the room with dignity. _____

EXERCISE B: Adding Transitive and Intransitive Verbs to Sentences. In each blank, write a verb that logically completes the sentence. In the blank after the sentence, write *I* (intransitive) or *T* (transitive) to describe the verb you wrote.

EXAMPLE: The harpist __*plucked*__ the shortest string. __*T*__

1. My parents _____ a new dresser for my bedroom. _____
2. The car _____ into the parking space easily. _____
3. A strong friendship _____ between the two families. _____
4. Benedict Arnold _____ the plans for West Point to the British. _____
5. The shop _____ beautiful floral centerpieces. _____
6. Please _____ those cabbages on the counter. _____
7. High winds _____ throughout the night. _____
8. The plane finally _____ after a three-hour delay. _____
9. The receptionist _____ another appointment in six weeks. _____
10. Linda _____ that article for the school paper. _____

1.3 Action Verbs and Linking Verbs

Linking Verbs

A linking verb is a verb that connects its subject with a word at or near the end of the sentence.

Forms of *Be* (from *Am* to *Would Have Been*)				Other Linking Verbs	
am	am being	can be	have been	appear	seem
are	are being	could be	has been	become	smell
is	is being	may be	had been	feel	sound
was	was being	might be	could have been	grow	stay
were	were being	must be	may have been	look	taste
		shall be	might have been	remain	turn
		should be	must have been		
		will be	shall have been		
		would be	should have been		
			will have been		
			would have been		

EXAMPLES: Ben should have been happy.   The friends stayed close for years.

Hudson's ship was the *Half Moon*.   The water in the pool *became* muddy.

EXERCISE A: Recognizing Forms of *Be* Used as Linking Verbs. Underline the linking verb in each sentence. Then circle the words that each verb links.

EXAMPLE: The Holts have been our neighbors for years.

1. Safety should be your first concern.
2. I would be happy to baby-sit for the Johnsons.
3. Elaine is often late for appointments.
4. Andrew can be an unusually stubborn child.
5. What could have been the cause of the accident?
6. That is a sufficient amount of sugar.
7. The setback was only temporary.
8. Surely Jenny will be our new class president.
9. Jason is being exceptionally polite today.
10. Thomas Jefferson was our third President.

EXERCISE B: Identifying Other Linking Verbs. Underline the linking verb in each sentence. Then circle the words that each verb links.

EXAMPLE: Rhoda became Mary's favorite friend.

1. Kevin appears taller on stage.
2. These sausages taste spicier than the last ones.
3. The cause of the accident remained a mystery.
4. That stranger looks suspicious.
5. The child stayed quiet throughout the doctor's examination.
6. The single white glove became the star's trademark.
7. A. A. Milne remains a popular children's author.
8. Sam's hair turned gray at an early age.
9. These old books smell musty.
10. I felt queasy during the boat ride.

1.3 Action Verbs and Linking Verbs

Linking Verb or Action Verb?

Some verbs may be used as an action verb in one sentence and as a linking verb in another. If a verb is a linking verb, *am, is,* or *are* will make sense when substituted for it in a sentence.

Linking Verbs	Action Verbs
The child *grew* very sleepy on the way home. (The child *is* very sleepy?) linking	Aunt Polly *grew* a prize-winning lily. (Aunt Polly *is* a prize-winning lily?) action

EXERCISE A: Distinguishing Between Linking Verbs and Action Verbs. On each blank at the right, write whether the sentence contains a linking verb or an action verb.

EXAMPLE: The milk turned sour. __*linking*__

1. The driver turned the corner too quickly. _____

2. The singer appeared slightly nervous. _____

3. After a half an hour, my date finally appeared. _____

4. I looked the robber directly in the face. _____

5. The table setting looks beautiful. _____

6. We all felt refreshed after a dip in the pool. _____

7. Dad finally felt the keys hidden under the car seat. _____

8. Donna's plan sounds excellent. _____

9. The principal sounded the fire alarm right after lunch. _____

10. Neville remained calm in spite of everything. _____

EXERCISE B: Adding Verbs to Sentences. Fill in each blank within the sentence with an appropriate verb. On the blank at the right, write *AV* for each action verb and *LV* for each linking verb.

EXAMPLE: Hungry people often __*become*__ irritable. __*LV*__

1. Litmus paper _____ blue in an alkaline solution. _____

2. Allison _____ the pages quickly, looking for the answer. _____

3. Johnson Farm _____ the best corn in the area. _____

4. The friends have _____ closer over the years. _____

5. Ronald Reagan _____ President in 1981. _____

6. The child's face _____ flushed. _____

7. _____ those facts up in an encyclopedia. _____

8. Have you ever _____ octopus? _____

9. Chocolate sauce _____ delicious on peppermint ice cream. _____

10. That music _____ much too loud. _____

1.4 | Helping Verbs

Recognizing Helping Verbs

Helping verbs are verbs that can be added to another verb to make a single verb phase. Any of the forms of *be* as well as some other common verbs can be used as helping verbs.

HELPING VERBS OTHER THAN *BE*			
do	have	shall	can
does	has	should	could
did	had	will	may
		would	might
			must

Finding Helping Verbs in Sentences

Other words may sometimes separate helping verbs from the key verb in a sentence.

Uninterrupted Verb Phrase	Interrupted Verb Phrase
We *will be visiting* you in July.	We *have* not yet *visited* the White House.

EXERCISE A: Identifying Helping Verbs. Underline each helping verb in the sentences below. Circle the key verb in the verb phrase.

EXAMPLE: Did anyone (call) for me?

1. Paul has not always acted so strangely.
2. Did Helen tell you about the party next week?
3. That student does not usually ride on this bus.
4. Have you ever traveled to Canada?
5. The driver must not have seen the stop sign.
6. Jason could have offered us his help.
7. Rehearsal should not have lasted so long.
8. I have seldom seen a more moving performance.
9. Mr. Wills does not always hear very well.
10. The plan could not have succeeded without your cooperation.

EXERCISE B: Adding Helping Verbs to Sentences. Fill in each blank with an appropriate helping verb. Circle each key verb.

EXAMPLE: When ___will___ the show (start)?

1. The woman at the information booth _____ answer that question.
2. I _____ _____ studying all week for that test.
3. Kyle _____ _____ seen that movie.
4. Someone _____ _____ _____ hurt.
5. What _____ you _____ doing all week?
6. _____ the art exhibit open on Saturday?
7. Some citizens _____ expressed reservations about the new bill.
8. The caller _____ _____ expected a more favorable response.
9. What time _____ the movie begin?
10. That construction crew _____ _____ working very hard.

2.1 Adjectives

The Process of Modification

An adjective is a word used to describe a noun or pronoun or to give a noun or pronoun a more specific meaning. Adjectives answer the question *What kind? Which one? How many?* or *How much?* about the nouns or pronouns they modify.

ADJECTIVE QUESTIONS		
What Kind?	*happy* child	*small* bird
Which One?	*next* room	*first* place
How Many?	*several* people	*three* days
How Much?	*little* work	*enough* money

EXERCISE A: Identifying Adjectives. Underline each adjective in the following sentences, including the articles *a, an,* and *the.* Then circle the noun or pronoun that each adjective modifies.

EXAMPLE: The tired horse pulled the heavy wooden wagon over the dirt road.

1. Several families had an outdoor party for the new neighbors.
2. The quaint and charming old house needed several major repairs.
3. The wealthy family had an extensive collection of antique glass.
4. The worthy cause drew many generous contributions.
5. At the end of the first round, Hawkins held a narrow lead.
6. Few people on that street have young children.
7. Western movies were popular for many years.
8. A good daily diet should include adequate calcium.
9. In many countries southern food is spicier than northern food.
10. The entire kingdom was under the terrible spell of the wicked sorcerer.

EXERCISE B: Adding Adjectives to Sentences. In each blank write an appropriate adjective that answers the question in parentheses.

EXAMPLE: ___Numerous___ ___younger___ families are moving into ___this___ area.
            (How many?)   (What kind?)   (Which one?)

1. The _____ shopper bought _____ pairs of shoes.
         (What kind?)   (How many?)

2. The _____ workers demanded _____ money.
         (What kind?)   (How much?)

3. _____ girl wore a _____ sweater like mine.
    (Which one?)   (What kind?)

4. The _____ guest at the _____ party wore jeans.
          (Which one?)   (What kind?)

5. _____ _____ _____ dogs howled.
    (How many?)   (What kind?)   (What kind?)

2.1 Adjectives

Proper and Compound Adjectives

A noun used as an adjective answers the question *What kind?* or *Which one?* about a noun that follows it.

Nouns	Nouns Used As Adjectives
automobile	automobile mechanic (*What kind* of mechanic?)
consumer	consumer reporter (*Which* reporter?)

Nouns Used As Adjectives

A compound adjective is an adjective that is made up of more than one word.

Hyphenated	Combined
upside-down cake	*upright* piano
full-scale rebellion	*keynote* speaker

A proper adjective is an adjective formed from a proper noun.

Proper Nouns	Proper Adjectives
Hawaii	*Hawaiian* pineapples
Athens	*Athenian* temple

EXERCISE A: Recognizing Nouns Used as Adjectives, Proper Adjectives, and Compound Adjectives. Identify the underlined adjectives in the sentences below as nouns used as adjectives, proper adjectives, or compound adjectives.

EXAMPLE: Our family enjoys eating in <u>Chinese</u> restaurants. _____*proper adjective*_____

1. The sitter read the child still another <u>bedtime</u> story. _____

2. The <u>overworked</u> secretary handed in his resignation. _____

3. Our class is visiting the <u>state</u> capital next week. _____

4. The bride wore a mantilla of <u>Spanish</u> lace. _____

5. We always use the good dishes for our <u>holiday</u> meals. _____

6. The concert was held in a <u>downtown</u> park. _____

7. Grandma made a <u>peach</u> cobbler for dessert. _____

8. The town finally rebelled against the <u>back-room</u> politics. _____

9. <u>Edwardian</u> clothing is enjoying a vogue. _____

10. I know the star of that <u>Broadway</u> play. _____

EXERCISE B: Using Proper and Compound Adjectives to Modify Nouns. Rewrite each word group below, placing a proper adjective or compound adjective before the main noun.

EXAMPLE: tenor from Italy _____*Italian tenor*_____

1. fishing in the deep sea _____

2. sale on a sidewalk _____

3. nation in Asia _____

4. poet from England _____

5. boy from a small town _____

6. villa in Rome _____

7. pool with salt water _____

8. rug from Persia _____

9. coffee from Turkey _____

10. seat in the front row _____

2.1 | Adjectives

Pronouns Used as Adjectives

A pronoun is used as an adjective if it modifies a noun. The chart below summarizes the kinds of pronouns used as adjectives and their use.

Possessive Adjectives		Demonstrative Adjectives	Interrogative Adjectives	Indefinite Adjectives			
				Singular	**Plural**	**Either**	
my	its	this	which	another	both	all	most
your	our	that	what	each	few	any	other
his	their	these	whose	either	many	more	some
her		those		neither	several		

Verbs Used as Adjectives

Verbs ending in *-ing* and *-ed* may sometimes be used as adjectives.

Verbs Used as Verbs	Verbs Used as Adjectives
Paul *is amusing* the children.	He told them an *amusing* story.
Karen *has broken* her ankle.	Her *broken* ankle is in a cast.

EXERCISE A: Adding Pronouns Used as Adjectives. Fill in each blank with the kind of pronoun given in parentheses.

EXAMPLE: Anita, ___*your*___ paper was excellent.   (possessive)

1. I have been wanting to read _____ book for a long time.   (demonstrative)

2. _____ students enjoy homework.   (indefinite)

3. _____ picture will look good over the mantel.   (indefinite)

4. I was uncertain about _____ pattern to choose.   (interrogative)

5. Mr. Parker always challenges _____ students.   (possessive)

6. In the summer, the Mannings have many parties beside _____ pool.   (possessive)

7. _____ contestant hoped to win.   (indefinite)

8. _____ homes in that part of town are very old.   (indefinite)

9. _____ math class will you be in?   (interrogative)

10. Are _____ chairs the ones we ordered?   (demonstrative)

EXERCISE B: Recognizing Verbs Used as Adjectives. In each sentence, underline the verb used as an adjective. Then circle the noun that it modifies.

EXAMPLE: The damp ground was the only reminder of the melted snow.

1. Dad replaced the shattered windowpane.
2. The screaming baby kept us awake all night.
3. In earlier times a mirror was called a looking glass.
4. We moved the fallen branch from the driveway.
5. By the time the police apprehended the burglars the stolen money had disappeared.
6. The freezing rain was the cause of the hazardous driving.
7. The winning car was powered by a large engine.
8. He arrived at the pool just in time to save a drowning boy.
9. The answers appear on the following pages.
10. The departing passengers checked in at the gate.

2.2 Adverbs

Adverbs Modifying Verbs, Adjectives, and Other Adverbs

An adverb is a word that modifies a verb, an adjective, or another adverb. An adverb answers one of four questions about the word it modifies: *Where? When? In what manner? To what extent?*

Adverbs Modifying Verbs	
drove *off* (Where?)	stayed *late* (When?)
ran *fast* (In what manner?)	*completely* missed (To what extent?)
Adverbs Modifying Adjectives	**Adverbs Modifying Adverbs**
rather special (To what extent?)	*not* really happy (To what extent?)

Nouns Used as Adverbs

Nouns used as adverbs answer the question *Where?* or *When?* about a verb.

Nouns	Adverbs
Today is my birthday.	The letter came *today*. (Came *when*?)
Their *home* is in Daytona.	David ran *home*. (Ran *where*?)

EXERCISE A: Recognizing Adverbs. Underline each adverb in the sentences below. Then circle the word it modifies.

EXAMPLE: That family just recently moved.

1. The snow melted quite rapidly last spring.
2. Clare has become a surprisingly good pianist.
3. That color suits you very well.
4. Mr. Whitkin seems somewhat dissatisfied with this assignment.
5. The careful attention to details insured a truly festive party.
6. We completed our chores fairly early.
7. I almost forgot what I wanted to ask you.
8. Our new house is very nearly ready.
9. The storm almost totally destroyed the railroad bridge.
10. That is an exceptionally clever design.

EXERCISE B: Identifying Adverbs and Nouns Used as Adverbs. Circle each noun used as an adverb. Underline all other adverbs.

EXAMPLE: The new play will open tomorrow.

1. The Joneses were not happy with their seat assignments.
2. What time did Danny come home?
3. This position is becoming increasingly uncomfortable.
4. Today will be a truly exciting day.
5. Our team won the big game yesterday.
6. Vinnie often works weekends.
7. The movers will be available Friday.
8. We were pleasantly surprised by their visit.
9. Shall we go to a movie tonight?
10. The silence grew somewhat awkward.

2.2 Adverbs

Adverb or Adjective?

Remember that an adverb modifies a verb, an adjective, or another adverb; an adjective modifies a noun or pronoun.

Adjectives	Adverbs
That train is *fast*.	A plane goes *fast*.
The *fast* train arrived on time.	An SST travels even *faster*.
Jackie is a *true* friend.	Jackie is *truly* kind.
Our case was *hopeless*.	We were *hopelessly* lost.

EXERCISE A: Distinguishing Between Adjectives and Adverbs. Write whether the underlined word in each sentence is an *adjective* or an *adverb*.

EXAMPLE: The dancer moved <u>gracefully</u>. _____adverb_____

1. The child looked <u>longingly</u> through the bakery window. _____
2. Kathy had always been an <u>early</u> riser. _____
3. Why did you come so <u>early</u>? _____
4. Kelly was the <u>only</u> person at home. _____
5. The baby is <u>only</u> six weeks old. _____
6. The accident could have been <u>fatal</u>. _____
7. Happily no one was <u>fatally</u> injured. _____
8. Josh swam <u>farther</u> out than the others. _____
9. The cabin is on the <u>farther</u> shore. _____
10. The neighbors became <u>close</u> friends. _____

EXERCISE B: Adding Adverbs and Adjectives to Sentences. If an adjective is needed in a sentence below, write the word in parentheses. If an adverb is needed, add *-ly* to the given word.

EXAMPLE: The little girl curtsied ___*gracefully*___. (graceful)

1. Most of my friends exercise _____ . (regular)
2. This muscle feels _____ from moving all that furniture. (sore)
3. We made a serious mistake but an _____ one. (honest)
4. The speaker considered her answer _____ . (careful)
5. We _____ go out to a movie on weekends. (frequent)
6. Uncle John is a _____ dinner guest at our house. (regular)
7. You can trust Ms. Franklin to answer your questions _____ . (honest)
8. Maria is usually a very _____ driver. (careful)
9. When the trip was canceled, the children were _____ disappointed. (sore)
10. Mr. O'Brien is a _____ visitor at our school. (frequent)

3.1 Prepositions

Words Used as Prepositions

A preposition is a word that relates a noun or pronoun following it to another word in the sentence.

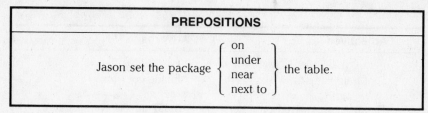

PREPOSITIONS

Jason set the package { on / under / near / next to } the table.

Prepositional Phases

A prepositional phrase is a group of words that begins with a preposition and ends with a noun or pronoun called the object of the preposition.

PREPOSITIONAL PHRASES	
Prepositions	Objects of Prepositions
between	*them*
around	the *museum*
on account of	the severe weather *conditions*

EXERCISE A: Supplying Prepositions. Fill in each blank with an appropriate preposition.

EXAMPLE: We completed the job _____*in spite of*_____ great difficulty.

1. The guests maintained constant chatter _____ the meal.
2. We found several valuable items _____ the clutter of the attic.
3. Trudy ordered a salad _____ the pizza.
4. The decorator placed the love seat _____ the wing chair.
5. The newscaster filed her report _____ the riots.
6. The guest speaker was delayed _____ heavy traffic.
7. The *Silver Meteor* arrived in New York _____ schedule.
8. You may substitute margarine _____ butter.
9. Everyone _____ Elsa enjoyed the boat ride.
10. _____ the large crowds, we enjoyed the art exhibit.

EXERCISE B: Identifying Prepositional Phrases. Bracket each prepositional phrase in the sentences below. Underline each preposition and circle its object. The number in parentheses tells how many phrases there are.

EXAMPLE: The doctor examined the patient [from (head)] [to (toe)].   (2)

1. According to the paper, the concert begins at dusk.   (2)
2. I saved a seat for you next to mine.   (2)
3. The headlines announced a truce between the two countries.   (1)
4. Cut two pounds of apples into quarter-inch slices.   (2)
5. A window with a northern exposure is perfect for that plant.   (2)
6. The passengers in the back of the boat got wet from the spray.   (3)
7. The hotel guests enter through a beautiful courtyard.   (1)
8. The house down the street has a weathervane on the top of its garage.   (3)
9. We looked into the abandoned house through a crack in the window.   (3)
10. Ted found the map underneath the woodpile behind the barn.   (2)

3.1 | Prepositions

Preposition or Adverb?

Many words can be either a preposition or an adverb, depending on how they are used. Remember that prepositions always have objects. Adverbs do not.

Prepositions	Adverbs
Sauté the onions *in* butter.	Please let the cat *in*.
Willie ran *through* the town.	These shades let some light *through*.

EXERCISE A: Distinguishing Between Prepositions and Adverbs. Write whether the underlined word in each sentence is a preposition or an adverb.

EXAMPLE: The desk has drawers on the bottom and shelves <u>above</u>. __*adverb*__

1. Once inside, we took our jackets <u>off</u>. _____
2. Last weekend my parents moved the living-room furniture <u>around</u>. _____
3. The splinter is just <u>below</u> the surface of the skin. _____
4. Just set the package <u>inside</u> the garage. _____
5. Distribute the raisins evenly <u>throughout</u>, please. _____
6. The executive's remarks were made <u>off</u> the record. _____
7. Sign your name in the space <u>below</u>. _____
8. When the drizzle began, we moved our picnic <u>inside</u>. _____
9. We planted marigolds <u>around</u> the vegetable garden. _____
10. The sirens could be heard <u>throughout</u> the town. _____

EXERCISE B: Adding Prepositions and Adverbs to Sentences. Fill in a word that is appropriate for the meaning of both sentences in each pair. In the sentence in which the word is used as a preposition, circle its object.

EXAMPLE: a. I had never seen the Statue of Liberty __*before*__.
   b. Please set the table __*before*__ (dinner.)

1. a. The cake has two layers with jelly _____.
   b. The Delaware River forms a lengthy boundary _____ two states.
2. a. This sweater was made _____ hand.
   b. When will the parade pass _____?
3. a. Did you remember to turn the oven _____?
   b. Hannah put a twenty-cent stamp _____ the envelope.
4. a. The owners converted the barn _____ the house into apartments.
   b. The puppy tagged along _____.
5. a. Turn right just _____ the library.
   b. The runner had gone _____ before we knew it.

3.2 Conjunctions and Interjections

Different Kinds of Conjunctions

A conjunction is a word used to connect other words or groups of words. Coordinating and correlative conjunctions join similar kinds of words or groups of words that are grammatically alike.

COORDINATING CONJUNCTIONS						
and	but	for	nor	or	so	yet

CORRELATIVE CONJUNCTIONS		
both . . . and	neither . . . nor	whether . . . or
either . . . or	not only . . . but also	

Subordinating conjunctions connect two complete ideas by making one subordinate to, or less important than, the other.

FREQUENTLY USED SUBORDINATING CONJUNCTIONS			
after	because	now that	until
although	before	since	when
as	even if	so that	whenever
as if	even though	than	where
as long as	if	though	wherever
as soon as	in order that	till	while
as though	lest	unless	

EXERCISE A: Identifying Conjunctions. Underline the conjunction in each sentence. Then write whether it is coordinating, correlative, or subordinating.

EXAMPLE: This restaurant is <u>not only</u> elegant <u>but also</u> expensive. _____*correlative*_____

1. I had not finished the dishes before the visitors arrived. _____

2. The lines of that dress are simple yet elegant. _____

3. The child was cooperative but wary during the examination. _____

4. The soup needs both salt and pepper. _____

5. I mentally outlined my essay while I waited for the bus. _____

6. The last problem on the test was harder than the others were. _____

7. Neither the hosts nor the guests had a very good time. _____

8. Grandma sat with the baby until he went to sleep. _____

9. Please finish packing your suitcase so that we can load the car. _____

10. Terry jumps up whenever anyone rings the doorbell. _____

EXERCISE B: Adding Conjunctions in Sentences. Fill in the blanks with an appropriate conjunction of the kind given in parentheses.

EXAMPLE: Alison offered to help, ____*but*____ the offer came too late.   (coordinating)

1. _____ you finish your chores, I will be waiting for you.   (subordinating)

2. Voting is _____ a right _____ a duty.   (correlative)

3. Elaine was uncertain _____ willing to try the snails.   (coordinating)

4. You must hurry, _____ we will surely be late.   (coordinating)

5. _____ the players were disappointed, they were good sports.   (subordinating)

3.2 | Conjunctions and Interjections

Conjunction, Preposition, or Adverb?

A few words can be conjunctions, prepositions, or adverbs. Remember that conjunctions always connect words or ideas.

SUBORDINATING CONJUNCTION
Since the Jacksons moved away, the neighborhood has been quieter.
PREPOSITION
I haven't seen Paul *since* breakfast.
ADVERB
Jim left town a week ago and hasn't been heard of *since*.

EXERCISE A: Identifying Words as Conjunctions, Prepositions, or Adverbs. Write whether each word underlined below is a conjunction, a preposition, or an adverb.

EXAMPLE: The game has been postponed <u>until</u> tomorrow. *preposition* .

1. <u>After</u> they returned from the lake, they began to think about dinner. _____

2. I know I have heard that song <u>before</u>. _____

3. Alex always does warm-up exercises <u>before</u> he begins jogging. _____

4. <u>After</u> dinner we played a trivia game. _____

5. <u>When</u> will dinner be ready? _____

6. Please put the toys away <u>when</u> you are finished with them. _____

7. <u>Until</u> I had seen the show myself, I couldn't understand the jokes. _____

8. Janice will wait for us <u>until</u> noon, and then she will leave. _____

9. Look <u>before</u> you leap. _____

10. The team has much work to do <u>before</u> the big game with Central High. _____

EXERCISE B: Adding Conjunctions, Prepositions, or Adverbs to Sentences. One word can be used to complete each set of sentences below. Fill in the blanks with the correct word. Then write *conjunction*, *preposition*, or *adverb* to tell how it is used in each sentence.

EXAMPLE: a. We had almost reached town _*when*_ we had a flat tire. _*conjunction*_
            b. _*When*_ did the alarm go off? _*adverb*_

1. a.   Have you ever eaten squid _____? _____

   b.   Jerry threw his warm-up pitches _____ the batter came up. _____

   c.   Snacks _____ meals can spoil your appetite. _____

2. a.   Several guests stayed _____ midnight. _____

   b.   You should not give your opinion _____ you have read the book. _____

3. a.   The yearbook staff will meet in the cafeteria _____ school. _____

   b.   Fran stayed to clean up _____ the party was over. _____

   c.   Mrs. Jenkins was grateful to the police ever _____. _____

4. a.   _____ Friday we have been waiting to hear the news. _____

   b.   _____ my grandmother came to visit, things have been very quiet. _____

3.2 Conjunctions and Interjections

Conjunctive Adverbs

A conjunctive adverb is an adverb that acts as a conjunction to connect complete ideas.

FREQUENTLY USED CONJUNCTIVE ADVERBS		
accordingly	finally	nevertheless
again	furthermore	otherwise
also	however	then
besides	indeed	therefore
consequently	moreover	thus

Interjections

An interjection is a word that expresses feeling or emotion and functions independently of a sentence.

SOME COMMON INTERJECTIONS		
aha	hey	tsk
alas	hurray	well
darn	oh	whew
goodness	ouch	wow

EXERCISE A: Recognizing Conjunctive Adverbs. Underline each conjunctive adverb in the sentences below. If a sentence does not have a conjunctive adverb, write *none* in the blank at the right.

EXAMPLE: Please open the door for me; my hands are full. ___*none*___

1. This apartment is quite roomy; besides, the price is right. _____

2. The star was taken ill suddenly; therefore, filming was delayed. _____

3. The bell rang early; school was dismissed. _____

4. Mr. Zims is a strict marker; indeed, he is strict in every way. _____

5. Grab your sweater; we've leaving right now. _____

6. James does not play tennis well; nevertheless, he is enthusiastic. _____

7. Mom checked the mouse traps; again, they were empty. _____

8. The crowd stood for the National Anthem; then, the game began. _____

9. These trees are deciduous; those are evergreens. _____

10. The river flooded many roads; consequently, traffic was rerouted. _____

EXERCISE B: Adding Interjections to Sentences. Fill in each blank with an interjection that shows the feeling or emotion given in parentheses.

EXAMPLE: ___*Darn*___! I was afraid that might happen. (annoyance)

1. _____ ! I burned my finger! (pain)

2. _____ , my favorite sweater shrank. (regret)

3. _____ ! Look at that rainbow! (delight)

4. _____ ! I never knew that. (surprise)

5. _____ ! This is some race. (excitement)

6. _____ ! I'm going to fall! (fear)

7. _____ ! I lost my keys again. (annoyance)

8. _____ ! It's another rainy day. (disappointment)

9. _____ ! The Bombers won! (enthusiasm)

10. _____ ! I'm ready for a break. (exhaustion)

4.1 | Words as Different Parts of Speech

Identifying Parts of Speech

The way a word is used in a sentence determines what part of speech it is.

DIFFERENT USES OF A WORD
As a Noun: The employees demanded more *pay*.
As a Verb: How much do the Johnsons *pay* their baby sitters?
As an Adjective: I can't wait for the next *pay* period to end.

EXERCISE A: Identifying Parts of Speech. On each blank at the right, write the name of the part of speech of the underlined word in the sentence.

EXAMPLE: a. <u>Next</u> Friday is Halloween. __*adjective*__

b. What shall we do <u>next</u>? __*adverb*__

1. a. The DeAngelos are having a <u>pool</u> party next weekend. _____

   b. Our neighbors have built a new <u>pool</u>. _____

2. a. The thieves <u>abandoned</u> their car on a side street. _____

   b. We found an old chest in the <u>abandoned</u> cabin. _____

3. a. I had not <u>thought</u> about Judy for a long time. _____

   b. Ken's only <u>thought</u> was for his own safety. _____

4. a. <u>Each</u> of the boys has his own room. _____

   b. We examined <u>each</u> peach for blemishes. _____

5. a. Big Ben is a famous <u>London</u> landmark. _____

   b. Our visit to <u>London</u> was a thrilling experience. _____

6. a. <u>Well</u>, what shall we have for dinner? _____

   b. The old <u>well</u> has dried up now. _____

7. a. That artist <u>sketches</u> with charcoal at country fairs. _____

   b. Many of Rembrandt's <u>sketches</u> are extremely valuable. _____

8. a. We cleaned up our camping area <u>before</u> we left. _____

   b. Mom jogs <u>before</u> breakfast every morning. _____

9. a. In the <u>fall</u>, that tree turns bright orange. _____

   b. How did you <u>fall</u> off the ladder? _____

10. a. Jesse tried <u>harder</u> than ever. _____

    b. This mattress is <u>harder</u> than the old one. _____

EXERCISE B: Using Words as Different Parts of Speech. Write a sentence for each word and part of speech given in parentheses.

EXAMPLE: a. (store, verb) __*Does the farmer store his corn in that silo?*__

b. (store, noun) __*That store is having a shoe sale.*__

1. a. (fast, noun) _____

   b. (fast, verb) _____

   c. (fast, adverb) _____

2. a. (by, preposition) _____

   b. (by, adverb) _____

5.1 Subjects and Verbs

Complete Subjects and Predicates

A sentence is a group of words with two main parts: a complete subject and a complete predicate. Together these parts express a complete thought.

Complete Subjects	Complete Predicates
Everyone on the team	tried hard.
The opposing players	did their best, too.
We	lost.

EXERCISE A: Recognizing Complete Subjects and Predicates. Draw a vertical line between each complete subject and predicate.

EXAMPLE: The runner in the green shirt | won.

1. Wild zebras roamed through the game preserve.
2. Elena did not allow enough time for the last essay question.
3. That game requires recalling a lot of trivial information.
4. That huge package in the hallway makes me curious.
5. The owners arranged a private tour for us.
6. The first zoo in the United States was in Philadelphia.
7. It continues to operate even today.
8. Children enjoy it immensely.
9. Rides on camels or elephants are available.
10. I accepted the invitation promptly.

EXERCISE B: More Work with Complete Subjects and Predicates. Follow the instructions in Exercise A.

EXAMPLE: The Pilgrims on the *Mayflower* | first landed at Provincetown.

1. That grapefruit tree in the corner grew from a seed ten years ago.
2. The stranger's behavior aroused the security guard's suspicion.
3. Male and female crocodiles carry their young in their mouths.
4. Hieroglyphics were the picture writings of the ancient Egyptians.
5. Spectators applauded with great enthusiasm.
6. A small ferry boat takes passengers on cruises around the islands.
7. Thanksgiving Day is always on the fourth Thursday in November.
8. Pumpkin pie is my favorite desert.
9. Automobile safety belts save thousands of lives every year.
10. Jeremy phoned home after school.

5.1 | Subjects and Verbs

Sentence or Fragment?

A fragment is a group of words that does not express a complete thought.

Fragments	Complete Sentences
Over the weekend.	What did you do over the weekend?
Each of the judges.	Each of the judges had a different opinion.
Made its home under the woodpile.	A small brown toad made its home under the woodpile.

EXERCISE A: Distinguishing Between Sentences and Fragments. In the blanks below, write *S* for each sentence and *F* for each fragment.

EXAMPLE: Within minutes after the call. __*F*__

1. In spite of Susanna's objections. _____
2. Hot dogs and hamburgers were on the grill. _____
3. Amanda helped. _____
4. Throughout the summer. _____
5. Inspector Snootch followed his hunch. _____
6. Visitors from near and far. _____
7. The player with the highest batting average in the league. _____
8. Spends several hours a week on her hobby. _____
9. The whale appeared. _____
10. A bat does not have true wings. _____

EXERCISE B: Writing Sentences from Fragments. Rewrite five of the items labeled *F* above as complete sentences.

EXAMPLE: The emergency crew arrived within minutes after the call.

1. _____

   _____

2. _____

   _____

3. _____

   _____

4. _____

   _____

5. _____

   _____

5.1 Subjects and Verbs

Simple Subjects and Predicates

The simple subject is the essential noun, pronoun, or group of words acting as a noun that cannot be left out of the complete subject. The simple predicate is the essential verb or verb phrase that cannot be left out of the complete predicate. In the chart below, the simple subjects are underlined once and the simple predicates are underlined twice.

Complete Subjects	Complete Predicates
Looking worried, <u>Tom</u>	<u><u>tried</u></u> the phone call again.
<u>Most</u> of us	<u><u>thought</u></u> the movie was boring.
Many <u>citizens</u> in this country	<u><u>do</u></u> not <u><u>vote</u></u>.
<u>Sheryl</u>	<u><u>called</u></u>.

In the third example above, notice that a word that interrupts the verb phrase is not part of the simple predicate.

EXERCISE A: Recognizing Simple Subjects and Predicates. Draw a line between the complete subject and complete predicate in each sentence. Then underline each simple subject and predicate.

EXAMPLE: <u>Each</u> of my friends | <u><u>has</u></u> an entirely different personality.

1. Many of the photographs had become brittle with age.
2. We enjoyed the picnic in spite of the showers.
3. The organizers of the event were unhappy with the turnout.
4. The sound of emergency vehicles pierced the night.
5. All of the members of that group wear outrageous clothing.
6. You promised me another chance.
7. A few of the committee members did not attend.
8. A number of beachfront properties were destroyed by the hurricane.
9. Who volunteered for the clean-up committee?
10. Mom had not ordered the curtains yet.

EXERCISE B: Adding Sentence Parts. Each word group below is missing either a complete subject or a complete predicate. Write a missing part to create a complete sentence. Then circle each simple subject and simple predicate.

EXAMPLE: _The guest (speaker) at the banquet_ (was) the governor.

1. _____ reads several books a week.
2. _____ receives a friendly welcome.
3. No one in my homeroom _____.
4. _____ bats left-handed.
5. The chef in that restaurant _____.
6. _____ arrived in record time.
7. _____ are elected to six-year terms.
8. Every member of the club _____.
9. The nickname of our state _____.
10. Most of the animals in the circus _____.

5.1 Subjects and Verbs

Compound Subjects and Verbs

A compound subject is two or more subjects that have the same verb and are joined by a conjunction such as *and* or *or*. A compound verb is two or more verbs that have the same subject and are joined by a conjunction such as *and* or *or*.

COMPOUND SUBJECT
Henry, Florence, and the Broudys spent their vacation together.
COMPOUND VERB
The storm continued and worsened throughout the night.

EXERCISE A: Recognizing Compound Subjects. Underline the nouns or pronouns that make up each compound subject below.

EXAMPLE: The pitcher and the catcher must have good communication.

1. Neither Jake nor I understood the problem.
2. The President and the Vice President rode in separate cars.
3. The Senate, the House of Representatives, and the Supreme Court assemble for the State of the Union Address.
4. Not only the guests but also the hosts enjoyed the party.
5. Both lilacs and roses are highly scented flowers.
6. Shrimp and other shellfish are good sources of iodine.
7. Oranges, lemons, limes, and grapefruits are citrus fruits.
8. Paul and I loved our new bunk beds.
9. The museum guide or one of the guards should be able to direct you.
10. Measles and mumps have been nearly eliminated by vaccines.

EXERCISE B: Recognizing Compound Verbs. Underline the verbs that make up each compound verb below.

EXAMPLE: The sales representative opened her bag and began her talk.

1. The plane touched the ground and glided to a stop.
2. Amanda did not give up but practiced her music even harder.
3. Joe writes with his right hand but bats with his left.
4. Ginny often writes or calls home from college.
5. Kelly added the vegetables, adjusted the seasoning, and turned the soup down to a simmer.
6. The audience clapped, cheered, and called for an encore.
7. Jessica put down her book and yawned.
8. Pam checked the card catalog but found few books on her topic.
9. The clematis overgrew the trellis and began climbing the chimney.
10. The troops neither retreated nor surrendered.

Hard-to-Find Subjects

Subjects in Orders and Directions

In sentences that give orders or directions, the subject is understood to be *you*. Notice that this is true even when a person is addressed by name.

Orders or Directions	With Subjects Added
After dinner, please wash the dishes.	After dinner, (you) please wash the dishes.
Just put the box over there.	(You) just put the box over there.
Andy, pass in your paper.	Andy, (you) pass in your paper.

Subjects in Inverted Sentences

In questions, the subject often follows the verb. To find the subject, mentally rephrase the question.

Question	Rephrased as Statement
<u>Did</u> the <u>bus</u> <u>leave</u>?	The <u>bus</u> <u>did leave</u>.

The subject of a sentence is never *there* or *here*. Like inverted questions, such sentences can usually be rephrased as statements to find the subject.

Sentence Beginning with *There* or *Here*	Rephrased with Subject First
There <u>is</u> the lost <u>puppy</u>.	The lost <u>puppy</u> <u>is</u> there.

In some sentences the subject is placed after the verb in order to receive greater emphasis. Such sentences can be mentally rephrased in normal subject-verb order to find the subject.

Inverted Word Order	Rephrased in Subject-Verb Order
Outside the door <u>was</u> a <u>package</u>.	A <u>package</u> <u>was</u> outside the door.

EXERCISE A: Finding Subjects in Orders or Directions. Write the subject of each sentence in the blank at the right. Put a caret (ʌ) where the subject belongs in the sentence.

EXAMPLE: Simon, ʌ take this note to the office. ___*(you)*___

1. After the third traffic light, turn right. _____

2. Erica, let me see your needlepoint. _____

3. Remember to feed the cat. _____

4. Tonight read the first two chapters of *Moby Dick*. _____

5. Jodi, remind me to bring my camera. _____

EXERCISE B: Finding Subjects in Inverted Sentences. Underline the subject in each sentence.

EXAMPLE: Here is your <u>essay</u>.

1. Into the burning building rushed the firefighters.
2. How can we ever find our way out of here?
3. Somewhere between the two extremes lies the best solution.
4. There are two errors in this report.
5. Beyond the stream bloomed a multitude of wildflowers.

5.3 Direct Objects, Indirect Objects, and Objective Complements

The Direct Object

A complement is a word or group of words that completes the meaning of the predicate of a sentence. A direct object is a noun or pronoun that receives the action of a transitive action verb.

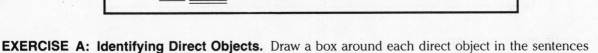

```
                        DIRECT OBJECTS
                            DO
        The nurse aroused the patient. (aroused whom? patient)
            DO        DO
        I ordered ham and eggs. (ordered what? ham and eggs)
                    PREP PHRASE
        Alice studied for three hours. (studied what? no answer)
```

EXERCISE A: Identifying Direct Objects. Draw a box around each direct object in the sentences below.

EXAMPLE: We planted peas, beans, and carrots in our garden.

1. We usually change the sheets on Monday.
2. That author has published a novel and several magazine articles.
3. The three students took a bus to the museum.
4. You could ask the doorkeeper for directions.
5. Carol asked the teacher for an extension on her term paper.
6. You can follow either State Street or High Road to the fair grounds.
7. The florist used daffodils and other spring flowers in the arrangement.
8. We need an interesting fabric for the pillows.
9. Paula borrowed my notes before the test.
10. They sell only three different kinds of ice cream.

EXERCISE B: More Work with Direct Objects. Each sentence below contains an action verb, some transitive and some intransitive. Draw a box around each direct object after a transitive verb. Underline any prepositional phrases.

EXAMPLE: The train screeched to a stop.

1. The children played board games for hours.
2. The cat played with a ball of yarn.
3. Everyone enjoyed the party.
4. Queen Anne's lace grew by the side of the road.
5. That restaurant serves only steaks and seafood.
6. The chef prepares everything with great care.
7. The actor moved in front of the camera.
8. The driver moved the car to a shadier spot.
9. Hillary has never ridden a horse before.
10. The cowboy has ridden out of town.

5.3 | Direct Objects, Indirect Objects, and Objective Complements

The Indirect Object

An indirect object is a noun or pronoun that appears with a direct object and names the person or thing that something is given to or done for.

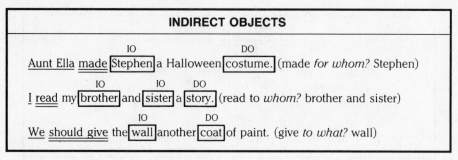

The Objective Complement

An objective complement is an adjective or noun that follows a direct object and describes or renames it.

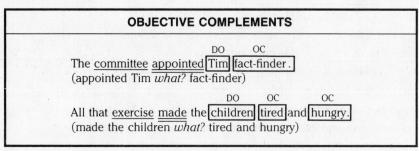

EXERCISE A: Identifying Indirect Objects. Underline each indirect object in the sentences below.

EXAMPLE: Sue showed <u>Tom</u> and <u>me</u> the pictures from her trip.

1. Grandma brought Michelle and Joe new bathing suits.
2. The prisoner finally told his lawyer the whole story.
3. Ellis offered each guest a tour of the mansion.
4. Has Jenkins shown the police the evidence?
5. The judges awarded Kelly a blue ribbon for her prize heifer.
6. Tess passed Helen and Kim a message in code.
7. The chess master showed Boris a new opening move.
8. Did you leave Mom and Dad a note?
9. Danny wrote Aunt Helen a warm thank-you note.
10. Uncle Dave taught me the breast stroke.

EXERCISE B: Recognizing Objective Complements. Underline each objective complement in the sentences below. Then write whether it is a noun or an adjective.

EXAMPLE: The last scene left the audience <u>frightened</u>. _____adjective_____

1. The dessert made the meal very satisfying. _____
2. The club elected Susan treasurer. _____
3. The judge declared the complaint invalid. _____
4. The new game kept everyone busy for hours. _____
5. The family called the new puppy Toby. _____

5.4 Subject Complements

The Predicate Nominative

There are two different kinds of subject complements: predicate nominatives and predicate adjectives. A predicate nominative is a noun or pronoun that follows a linking verb and renames, identifies, or explains the subject of the sentence.

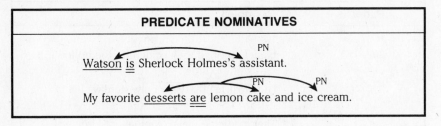

Predicate Adjectives

A predicate adjective is an adjective that follows a linking verb and describes the subject of the sentence.

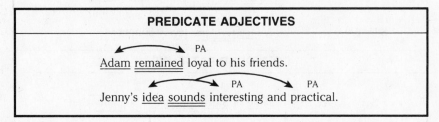

EXERCISE A: Recognizing Predicate Nominatives and Predicate Adjectives. Underline each subject complement in the sentences below. Then identify each as either a PA (predicate adjective) or a PN (predicate nominative).

EXAMPLE: The baby's best friends are his <u>blanket</u> and his <u>teddy bear</u>. ___*PN*___

1. After the race, the runners felt tired but exhilarated. _____

2. Janet became tan and muscular during her month at camp. _____

3. That novel became an overnight best-seller. _____

4. The singer's albums are as popular now as ever. _____

5. A straight line is the shortest distance between two points. _____

6. The retired officer remained a consultant on special projects. _____

7. Paula, Pam, and Patty are triplets. _____

8. Barbara will become either a surgeon or an internist. _____

9. The police search was extremely thorough. _____

10. Jim's suggestion was neither constructive nor workable. _____

EXERCISE B: Writing Sentences with Compound Subject Complements. Each sentence below contains a subject complement. On the first line, add a second subject complement. Then identify each as a *PA* (predicate adjective) or a *PN* (predicate nominative).

EXAMPLE: That sentence is unclear and ___*uninteresting*___. ___*PA*___

1. Anita's suggestion was tactful and _____. _____

2. Some sauces are both rich and _____. _____

3. Not all writers become famous and _____. _____

4. The teams in the finals will be the Majors and the _____. _____

5. The co-captains are Sandy and _____.

5.5 | Basic Sentence Patterns

Basic Sentence Patterns

In the English language, subjects, verbs, and complements follow five basic sentence patterns.

PATTERNS WITH TRANSITIVE VERBS	
Patterns	**Examples**
S-AV-DO	Lionel reported the [accident] to the police. (DO)
S-AV-IO-DO	Lucy read [me] her [speech] yesterday. (IO, DO)
S-AV-DO-OC	That medicine makes the [patient] [drowsy.] (DO, OC)
PATTERNS WITH LINKING VERBS	
S-LV-PN	Lincoln became [President] in 1861. (PN)
S-LV-PA	My face turns [red] every summer. (PA)
COMPOUND PATTERNS	
S-S-AV-DO-AV-DO	Elaine or Steve will water the [plants] and feed the [fish.] (DO, DO)
S-LV-PA-PA	This book smells [old] and [musty.] (PA, PA)

EXERCISE A: Recognizing the Parts of Basic Sentence Patterns. Underline each subject once and each verb twice. Draw a box around each complement.

EXAMPLE: The critic called the [food] [bland] and [uninteresting.]   _____

1. The guide showed us a new route. _____
2. Neither Jack nor Joan had visited us recently. _____
3. The artist's work is detailed and delicate. _____
4. Amanda felt discouraged by the defeat. _____
5. Victoria became Queen in 1837. _____
6. The graduates began the ceremonies with a song. _____
7. The director sent us a brochure about the camp. _____
8. Dora gave a huge party for the class. _____
9. Mme. Hulot's inspiration made me an avid student of French literature. _____
10. Dad promised Hugh and me a bonus for our yard work. _____

EXERCISE B: Recognizing Basic Sentence Patterns. Write the pattern of each sentence in Exercise A, using the lines to the right of the sentences.

EXAMPLE: The critic called the [food] [bland] and [uninteresting.]   *S-AV-DO-OC-OC*

5.5 Basic Sentence Patterns

Inverted Patterns

In an inverted sentence pattern, the subject is never first.

PATTERNS FOR QUESTIONS	
Patterns	**Examples**
V-S	How <u>are</u> <u>you</u>?
HV-S-V	<u>Are</u> <u>you</u> <u>coming</u> along?
V-S-COMP	<u>Was</u> <u>Pete</u> the [speaker]^{PN}?
HV-S-V-COMP	<u>Have</u> <u>you</u> <u>written</u> your [essay]^{DO}?
COMP-HV-S-V	[What]^{DO} <u>are</u> <u>you</u> <u>doing</u>?

PATTERNS FOR SENTENCES BEGINNING WITH *THERE* OR *HERE*	
V-S	There <u>is</u> little <u>hope</u> of success.

PATTERNS FOR SENTENCES INVERTED FOR EMPHASIS	
V-S	All around us <u>was</u> <u>wilderness</u>.
COMP-S-V	What a catch the <u>shortstop</u> <u>made</u>!^{DO}
COMP-V-S	How mysterious <u>seemed</u> the <u>stranger</u>!^{PA}

EXERCISE A: Recognizing the Parts of Inverted Sentence Patterns. Underline each subject once and each verb twice. Draw a box around each complement.

EXAMPLE: Where <u>did</u> <u>you</u> <u>put</u> yesterday's [paper]? _____

1. How eager we were for a win! _____
2. There is a very good chance of rain tomorrow. _____
3. What courses will you be taking? _____
4. Has Gerry prepared her speech yet? _____
5. What majestic mountains those are! _____
6. Am I the only one here? _____
7. Here are some more books by that author. _____
8. Out of the barn bolted the stallion. _____
9. Was the play successful? _____
10. From inside the house came a loud shriek. _____

EXERCISE B: Recognizing Inverted Sentence Patterns. Write the pattern of each sentence in Exercise A, using the lines to the right of the sentences.

EXAMPLE: Where <u>did</u> <u>you</u> <u>put</u> yesterday's [paper]?   *HV-S-V-COMP*

5.6 Diagraming Basic Sentence Parts

Subjects, Verbs, and Modifiers

In a sentence diagram, the subject and verb are written on a horizontal line with the subject on the left and the verb on the right. A vertical line separates the subject and verb. Adjectives and adverbs are placed on slanted lines directly below the words that they modify.

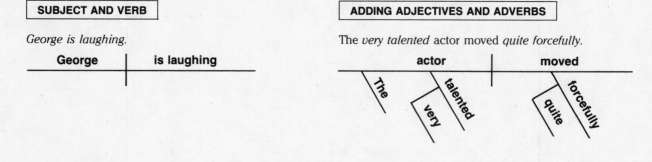

SUBJECT AND VERB

George is laughing.

ADDING ADJECTIVES AND ADVERBS

The *very talented* actor moved *quite forcefully*.

Orders and directions whose subject is understood to be *you* are diagramed in the usual way with parentheses around the understood subject. Inverted sentences are diagramed following the usual subject-verb order, with the capital letter indicating which word begins the sentence.

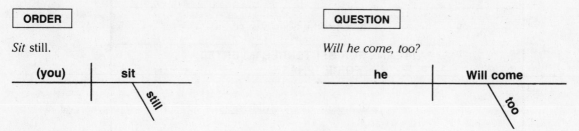

ORDER

Sit still.

QUESTION

Will he come, too?

Diagram expletives, interjections, and nouns of direct address by placing them on horizontal lines above the subject.

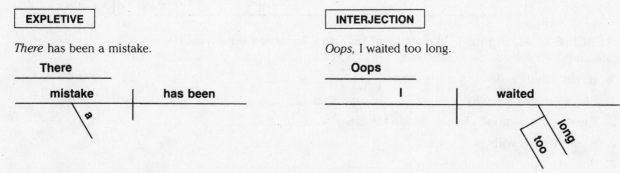

EXPLETIVE

There has been a mistake.

INTERJECTION

Oops, I waited too long.

EXERCISE A: Diagraming Subjects, Verbs, and Modifiers. Correctly diagram each sentence. Refer to the samples above if you need to.

1. Beautiful wildflowers grew everywhere.

2. The old dirt road curved sharply.

EXERCISE B: More Work with Diagrams. Correctly diagram each sentence.

1. Will the circus parade pass here?

2. Move over.

3. Here is the answer.

5.6 | Diagraming Basic Sentence Parts

Adding Conjunctions

Conjunctions are diagramed on dotted lines drawn between the words they connect.

ADDING CONJUNCTIONS

The sleek *but* powerful deer ran quickly *and* gracefully.

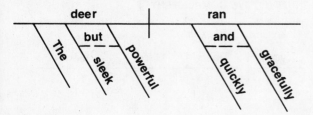

Conjunctions that connect compound subjects and compound verbs are also written on dotted lines between the words they connect.

COMPOUND SUBJECT

Many happy *children* and unhappy *adults* are arriving.

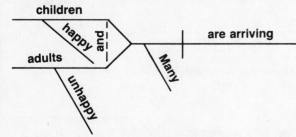

COMPOUND VERB

The Hollands *came* early and *stayed* late.

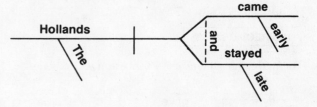

EXERCISE A: Diagraming Sentences with Conjunctions.
Diagram each sentence correctly. Refer to the examples above if you need to.

1. The powerful and ruthless tyrant was assassinated.

2. The strong but graceful athlete moved rapidly and effortlessly.

EXERCISE B: More Work with Diagraming.
Correctly diagram each sentence.

1. Sandy and Dennis have never sung together.

2. The committee met frequently and planned very carefully.

3. Many willing and eager volunteers are working hard.

5.6 Diagraming Basic Sentence Parts

Complements

In diagrams, most complements are placed on the base line after the verb. A straight line that meets the base line separates a direct object from the verb. A slanted line that meets the base line comes before an objective complement or a subject complement. An indirect object is joined to the rest of the sentence below each verb. Compound complements are joined as other compound parts.

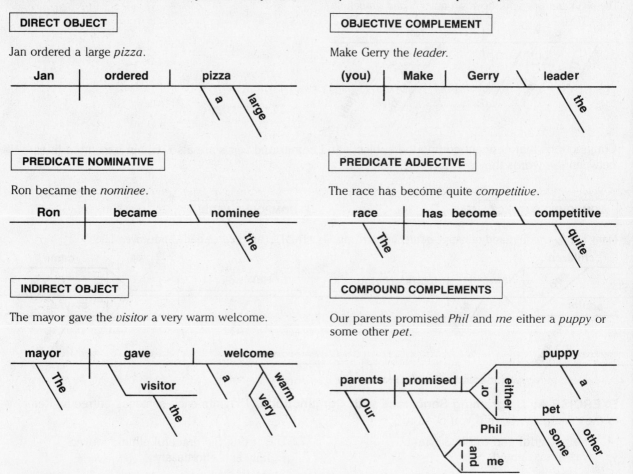

DIRECT OBJECT

Jan ordered a large *pizza*.

OBJECTIVE COMPLEMENT

Make Gerry the *leader*.

PREDICATE NOMINATIVE

Ron became the *nominee*.

PREDICATE ADJECTIVE

The race has become quite *competitive*.

INDIRECT OBJECT

The mayor gave the *visitor* a very warm welcome.

COMPOUND COMPLEMENTS

Our parents promised *Phil* and *me* either a *puppy* or some other *pet*.

EXERCISE A: Diagraming Complements. Correctly diagram each sentence.

1. The police offered the informers immunity.

2. The referee declared the former champion the winner.

EXERCISE B: More Work with Complements. Correctly diagram each sentence.

1. Those children show their parents and other adults great respect.

2. Their new single quickly became a hit.

6.1 Prepositional Phrases

Adjective Phrases

A phrase is a group of words, without a subject and verb, that functions in a sentence as one part of speech. An adjectival phrase is a prepositional phrase that modifies a noun or pronoun by telling what kind or which one.

Adjectives	Adjective Phrases
These *dessert* plates are antiques.	These plates *for dessert* are antiques.
We defeated the *Boston* team.	We defeated the team *from Boston*.

Adverb Phrases

An adverb phrase is a prepositional phrase that modifies a verb, adjective, or adverb by pointing out where, when, in what manner, or to what extent.

Adverbs	Adverb Phrases
I packed *hastily*.	I packed *with great haste*.
The child was *irrationally* upset.	The child was upset *beyond reason*.
The band played *somewhat* louder.	The band played louder *to some extent*.

EXERCISE A: Identifying Adjective Phrases. Underline each adjective phrase in the sentences below. Circle the noun or pronoun it modifies.

EXAMPLE: The maple (tree) in the back yard is (one) of my favorite trees.

1. Everyone in the lab completed the experiment on page 30.
2. The new house at the end of the street is nearly finished.
3. The gate in the fence around the estate was padlocked.
4. Tomorrow the mayor will announce her plans for the new committee.
5. Exchange students from France are visiting a family in our neighborhood.

EXERCISE B: Identifying Adverb Phrases. Underline each adverb phrase in the sentence below. Circle the verb, adjective, or adverb it modifies.

EXAMPLE: Without a word to anyone, John (walked) out of the house.

1. The nervous applicant shifted from one foot to the other.
2. Without any hesitation, Frank stepped to the microphone.
3. No unauthorized personnel was permitted close to the launch pad.
4. After the game we stopped at the diner on Hudson Street.
5. Hundreds of fans were eager for a glimpse of the star.

6.2 Appositives and Appositive Phrases

Appositives

An appositive is a noun or pronoun placed next to another noun or pronoun to identify or explain it.

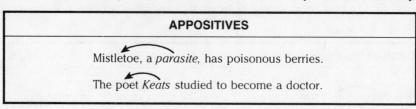

APPOSITIVES
Mistletoe, a *parasite*, has poisonous berries.
The poet *Keats* studied to become a doctor.

Appositive Phrases

An appositive phrase is a noun or pronoun with modifiers, placed next to a noun or pronoun to add information and details.

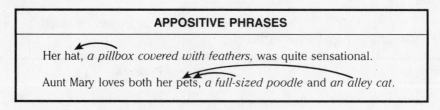

APPOSITIVE PHRASES
Her hat, *a pillbox covered with feathers,* was quite sensational.
Aunt Mary loves both her pets, *a full-sized poodle* and *an alley cat.*

EXERCISE A: Identifying Appositives and Appositive Phrases. Underline each appositive or appositive phrase in these sentences. Circle the noun or pronoun it renames.

EXAMPLE: Captain Ahab pursued (Moby Dick,) the great white whale.

1. Bastille Day, July 14, is the French Independence Day.
2. Only one person, either Juan or Linda, will get the job.
3. Kory had his standard lunch: tunafish with lettuce and cheese.
4. The safari stopped at an oasis, a moist, fertile spot in the desert.
5. The attorney handed Jenkins, her faithful clerk, a pile of briefs to file.
6. We all enjoyed ourselves.
7. The class agreed on two captains: Phyllis and Len.
8. Our new neighbors, a young couple from Paris, are quite friendly.
9. The class play will be the comedy *Arsenic and Old Lace.*
10. All of them, Pete, Sue, and Judy, tried out for parts.

EXERCISE B: Writing Sentences with Appositives and Appositive Phrases. Turn each pair of sentences into a single sentence by adding one or more appositives or appositive phrases.

EXAMPLE: We served a traditional St. Patrick's Day dinner. It was corned beef and steamed cabbage.
We served a traditional St. Patrick's Day dinner: corned beef and steamed cabbage.

1. The explorers opened the Northwest Territory. They were Lewis and Clark.

_____

2. Delaware has only three counties. They are Kent, Sussex, and New Castle.

_____

3. My cousin lives in Austin. It is the capital of Texas.

_____

4. A local reporter broke the story. She is Annette Jackson.

_____

5. Both finalists are fine competitors. They are Logan and Bruce.

_____

6.3 Participles and Participial Phrases

Participles

A participle is a form of a verb that can act as an adjective.

Present Participles	Past Participles
The runner, *panting*, waved to the *cheering* spectators.	The *broken* vase can be repaired by an *experienced* potter.

Verb or Participle?

A verb shows an action or condition. A participle acting as an adjective modifies a noun or a pronoun.

Verbs	Participles
The barometer is *falling*.	The *falling* barometer indicated a change.
Gunther *trained* the lion.	The *trained* lion went through the hoop.

EXERCISE A: Identifying Participles. Underline the participle in each sentence and circle the word it modifies. On the line at the right, write *present* or *past* to tell which kind it is.

EXAMPLE: Jessica is a spoiled (child.) __*past*__

1. Bob had a splint on his broken finger. _____
2. The sitter finally quieted the crying baby. _____
3. The crowd applauded the governor's stirring speech. _____
4. We put the injured bird in a shoe box. _____
5. I have never tried that frozen dessert. _____
6. Please send a copy to the acting chairman. _____
7. The lifeguard tried to save the drowning man. _____
8. Have you already applied for a building permit? _____
9. Louise regretted her broken promise. _____
10. The committee approved the revised proposal. _____

EXERCISE B: Distinguishing Between Verbs and Participles. On the line at the right, write whether each underlined word is a verb or a participle.

EXAMPLE: My favorite act was the dancing bear. __*participle*__

1. That noise is disturbing the neighbors. _____
2. I had a disturbing dream last night. _____
3. Can you repair this torn page? _____
4. Someone has torn all the coupons out of this magazine. _____
5. The opening chapter got off to a slow start. _____
6. Ron's play will be opening next week. _____
7. Are you laughing at me? _____
8. The laughing child got hiccups. _____
9. Please put these cut flowers in some water. _____
10. I cut my finger on a kitchen knife. _____

6.3 | Participles and Participial Phrases

Participial Phrases

A participial phrase is a participle modified by an adverb or adverb phrase or accompanied by a complement. The entire phrase acts as an adjective.

PARTICIPIAL PHRASES

The woman *playing the harp* is my aunt.

Feeling calmer, the driver explained what had happened.

The clerk *standing behind the counter* was helpful.

The person *coming out now* will do a solo.

Shaking hands warmly, the two candidates had made up their differences.

EXERCISE A: Recognizing Participial Phrases. Underline the participial phrase in each sentence. Then circle the word it modifies.

EXAMPLE: This (bread) made without preservatives, is delicious.

1. The family visiting the Jacksons once lived on this street.
2. A letter signed by Napoleon was found among the papers.
3. Feeling uneasy, the baby sitter checked all the locks.
4. Every pie sold at the farm store is baked on the premises.
5. Bought by an eccentric millionaire, the antique car will never run again.
6. Sylvia saw Mike standing outside the library.
7. Anyone having a pet is welcome to enter it in the show.
8. Confused by the directions, the contestant failed to answer.
9. That large plant hanging from the ceiling is a Boston fern.
10. The child, lost in the department store, became panicky.

EXERCISE B: Writing Sentences with Participial Phrases. Turn each pair of sentences into a single sentence with a participial phrase.

EXAMPLE: The enlargement was made from the negative. It was clearer than the original.
   The enlargement made from the negative was clearer than the original.

1. The person is looking in the window. It is our neighbor.

   _____

2. The storm is coming from the west. It is bringing precipitation.

   _____

3. Early sketches were made by that painter. They have become valuable.

   _____

4. The wallet was found on the street. It had no identification in it.

   _____

5. Food was served at the party. We all enjoyed the food.

   _____

6.3 | Participles and Participial Phrases

Nominative Absolutes

A nominative absolute is a noun or pronoun followed by a participle or participial phrase that functions independently of the rest of the sentence.

NOMINATIVE ABSOLUTES

Two weeks having gone by, our vacation was over. (time)

My grandmother being ill, we changed our plans. (reason)

The tide having just gone out, we got plenty of clams. (circumstance)

The power [being] off, we read by candlelight. (elliptical)

EXERCISE A: Recognizing Nominative Absolutes. Underline the nominative absolute in each sentence.

EXAMPLE: The players headed for the locker room, <u>the game over</u>.

1. The band continuing to play, diners stayed on to dance.
2. Hours having passed without any word, the family began to worry.
3. The patient recovering nicely, the doctor removed the no visitors order.
4. Janet took the exam orally, her right hand broken.
5. The team has lost three straight games, their best players injured.
6. Their chores completed, the children ran outside to play.
7. The train having broken down, commuters were bused to the next stop.
8. The buffet table looking so tempting, Sam went back for thirds.
9. Their argument resolved, the two friends went off arm in arm.
10. The air conditioning not working, the office closed at noon.

EXERCISE B: Writing Sentences with Nominative Absolutes. Rewrite each sentence below, adding a nominative absolute that gives the time, reason, or circumstance for the main statement.

EXAMPLE: The committee postponed the street fair.
The steady rain continuing, the committee postponed the street fair.

1. The police put up no-parking signs along the main street.

_____

2. The room looked very festive.

_____

3. Lucy was chilly at the picnic.

_____

4. We were able to borrow a bike for Kenny.

_____

5. The speaker was finally able to begin.

_____

6.4 Gerunds and Gerund Phrases

Gerunds

A gerund is a form of a verb that acts as a noun.

GERUNDS

Subject: *Jogging* is a popular exercise.
Direct Object: That device makes *driving* safer.
Indirect Object: Ellen gives *studying* her complete attention.
Predicate Nominative: Quentin's first love is *swimming*.
Object of a Preposition: The guests grew tired of *waiting*.
Appositive: Kathy is dedicated to her profession, *teaching*.

Verb, Participle, or Gerund?

Words ending in *-ing* that act as nouns are gerunds. They do not show an action, nor do they act as adjectives.

Verb	Participle	Gerund
Dad is *cooking* fish.	He took *cooking* lessons.	He enjoys *cooking*.

EXERCISE A: Recognizing Gerunds. Underline the gerund in each sentence. Then identify the use of each gerund, using one of these labels: *S* (subject), *DO* (direct object), *IO* (indirect object), *PN* (predicate nominative), *OP* (object of a preposition), or *APP* (appositive).

EXAMPLE: Mrs. Hill thanked us for helping.   ___OP___

1. Fishing can be a relaxing pastime.   _____

2. On rainy days, Andrew enjoys coloring.   _____

3. Erica is afraid of flying.   _____

4. Losing is never a happy experience.   _____

5. The teacher accused Gail of cheating.   _____

6. We looked forward to the main event, bowling.   _____

7. Pruning is important to the health of trees and shrubs.   _____

8. Les's favorite sport, skiing, is an expensive interest.   _____

9. Marge gives training six hours a day.   _____

10. Hank has shown no aptitude for drawing.   _____

EXERCISE B: Recognizing Verbs, Participles, and Gerunds. Write *V*, *P*, or *G* to indicate whether the underlined word in each sentence is a verb, a participle, or a gerund.

EXAMPLE: The team is hoping for a win.   ___V___

1. Ed never stopped hoping. _____

2. The gravy needs stirring. _____

3. Cal gave a stirring speech. _____

4. I was stirring the stew. _____

5. I have been shopping for
   new shoes. _____

6. Bruno hates shopping. _____

7. The shopping trip lasted all day. _____

8. Everyone was singing. _____

9. Jo practices singing daily. _____

10. Her singing teacher gives her
    great encouragement. _____

6.4 Gerunds and Gerund Phrases

Gerund Phrases

A gerund phrase is a gerund with modifiers or a complement, all acting together as a noun. In the chart, notice the words before the gerunds in the second and third examples. Remember that the possessive form of a noun or pronoun is used before a gerund.

GERUND PHRASES

S
Sleeping late is a luxury to many people.

PN
By far the biggest inconvenience was *the store's closing early*.

DO
Ann encouraged *our staying so long*.

OP
The guide helped by *giving us directions*.

EXERCISE A: Recognizing Gerund Phrases. Underline the gerund phrase in each sentence. Then tell whether each phrase is acting as a subject, predicate nominative, direct object, or object of a preposition, using the abbreviations in the chart.

EXAMPLE: The runner started for home without <u>tagging third base</u>.   _OP_

1. At the age of five, Pam began learning French. _____

2. My little brother's latest skill is counting to ten. _____

3. Training long hours is not unusual for an athlete. _____

4. Wilma kept changing her mind about the color for the walls. _____

5. Working for the mayor's re-election has been a learning experience. _____

6. Mom appreciated our working so hard. _____

7. The guard prevented us from entering the house. _____

8. The hardest part was choosing a good topic. _____

9. We still have hope of finding the buried treasure. _____

10. Marci became a superb pianist by practicing hard. _____

EXERCISE B: Writing Nouns and Pronouns Before Gerunds. Fill in each blank with the correct word form from the parentheses at the right.

EXAMPLE: _Your_   helping us out made the job easier.   (You, Your)

1. The team celebrated _____ winning the championship.   (they, their, them)

2. _____ playing of that piece was excellent.   (Suzi, Suzi's)

3. The audience applauded _____ singing of the duet.   (we, our, us)

4. _____ crying so long became annoying.   (He, His, Him)

5. _____ rising so early surprised my roommates.   (I, My, Me)

6. _____ becoming a dentist was a goal for years.   (She, Her)

7. _____ decorating the gym was a bad idea.   (They, Their, Them)

8. We were amazed at _____ diving off the high board.   (he, his, him)

9. The guests impatiently awaited _____ carving of the turkey.   (Ken, Ken's)

10. _____ buying the same outfit is a strange coincidence.   (You, Your)

6.5 | Infinitives and Infinitive Phrases

Infinitives

An infinitive is a form of a verb that generally appears with the word *to* and acts as a noun, adjective, or adverb.

INFINITIVES
Subject: To forgive takes understanding and generosity.
Direct Object: Warren offered *to help*.
Predicate Nominative: The team's desire was *to win*.
Object of a Preposition: We had no choice but *to follow*.
Appositive: Nina has one great desire, *to travel*.
Adjective: I am looking for something *to read*.
Adverb: This tool is easy *to use*.

Prepositional Phrase or Infinitive?

A prepositional phrase always ends with a noun or pronoun. An infinitive always ends with a verb.

Prepositional Phrase	Infinitive
We went *to Mexico* for vacation.	Is this a good place *to stand*?

EXERCISE A: Identifying Infinitives. Underline the infinitive in each sentence. Then tell whether it is being used as a noun, an adjective, or an adverb.

EXAMPLE: From here, the speaker is hard <u>to hear</u>. ___*adverb*___

1. Mrs. Link's advice was hard to accept. _____
2. Tom's willingness to work impressed his employer. _____
3. Is the Chinese language difficult to learn? _____
4. That plan is not likely to succeed. _____
5. New foods are often interesting to try. _____
6. Daedalus's great dream was to fly. _____
7. Hockey is an exciting sport to watch. _____
8. Hal's desire to rule has become an obsession. _____
9. In spite of the noise and confusion, we tried to listen. _____
10. The band finally began to play. _____

EXERCISE B: Distinguishing Between Prepositional Phrases and Infinitives. Write *PP* (prepositional phrase) or *INF* (infinitive) to describe each underlined group of words.

EXAMPLE: Dad went <u>to the market</u>. ___*PP*___

1. Is this the road <u>to take</u>? _____
2. Is this the road <u>to town</u>? _____
3. Fran walks <u>to school</u>. _____
4. Mom walks <u>to exercise</u>. _____
5. Just listen <u>to this</u>. _____
6. Pam is willing <u>to learn</u>. _____
7. Who is the one <u>to select</u>? _____
8. Hand this <u>to Kerry</u>. _____
9. This is important <u>to me</u>. _____
10. This is important <u>to know</u>. _____

6.5 Infinitives and Infinitive Phrases

Infinitive Phrases

An infinitive phrase is an infinitive with modifiers, complements, or a subject, all acting together as a single part of speech.

INFINITIVE PHRASES
DO We offered *to give them a hand*.
DO Have *June tell them the news*.
DO No one dared *speak above a whisper*.
S *To sit still* was hard for the child.

Notice that the infinitives in the second and third examples do not include the word *to*. When an infinitive or infinitive phrase is used as the direct object of certain verbs, *to* is often omitted.

EXERCISE A: Recognizing Infinitive Phrases. Underline the infinitive phrase in each sentence below. Then write the part of speech it is used as.

EXAMPLE: The candidate's promise, <u>to lower taxes</u>, won her the election. ___*noun*___

1. The coach's example is one to take seriously. _____

2. We all made an effort to work harder. _____

3. The contest requires all entries to be mailed by Thursday. _____

4. The players were eager to try on their new uniforms. _____

5. The director asked Mindy to audition for the part. _____

6. The children did not want to wait till dinnertime. _____

7. The innkeeper provided us with a place to spend the night. _____

8. This is the best place to find that game. _____

9. All of us will have to sell some of these tickets. _____

10. Vera's parents encouraged her to apply for the job. _____

EXERCISE B: More Work with Infinitive Phrases. Underline the infinitive phrase in each sentence. On the line at the right, write the infinitive itself. If *to* has been omitted, write it in parentheses.

EXAMPLE: Let <u>someone else have a turn</u>. ___*(to) have*___

1. We saw that team win the World Series. _____

2. The guide offered to show us an alternate route. _____

3. I have never heard him play that concerto before. _____

4. We watched the pitcher practice before the game. _____

5. We invited our cousins to come for the weekend. _____

6. No one would dare disagree with the President in public. _____

7. Can't we make you stay for dinner? _____

8. Please bring an inexpensive, humorous gift. _____

9. The candidate's family encouraged her to run again. _____

10. Let's take a break from raking these leaves. _____

6.6 Diagraming Phrases

Prepositional Phrases

A prepositional phrase is diagramed to show how it relates the object of the preposition to another word in the sentence. The preposition is written on a slanted line joined to the word the phrase modifies. The object is written on a horizontal line. Modifiers are diagramed as usual.

ADJECTIVE PHRASES

A man *with a slight limp* was whistling a song *from a play*.

ADVERB PHRASES

A vase full *of fresh tulips and daisies* was delivered *on Monday*.

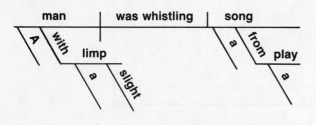

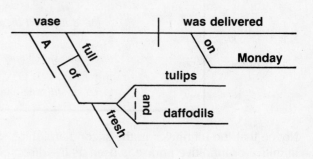

Appositives and Appositive Phrases

An appositive is diagramed in parentheses next to the noun or pronoun it renames. Any modifiers are diagramed in the usual way.

APPOSITIVE

My sister's friend *Linda* is a law student.

APPOSITIVE PHRASE

We greatly enjoyed the movie, *a comedy with music*.

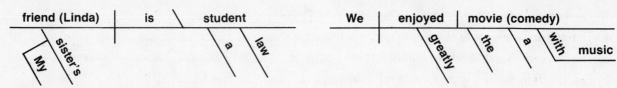

EXERCISE A: Diagraming Prepositional Phrases. Correctly diagram each sentence. Refer to the models above if necessary.

1. Someone from the agency called you about your tickets.

2. The doll in the window of the shop was bought for a wealthy little girl.

EXERCISE B: Diagraming Appositives and Appositive Phrases. Correctly diagram each sentence. Refer to the models if necessary.

1. Doug finally achieved his dream, a house near the ocean.

2. The employer gave Connie, a very hard worker, more responsibility.

6.6 Diagraming Phrases

Participles and Participial Phrases

The diagram for a participle or a participial phase looks much like the diagram for a prepositional phrase below the noun or pronoun it modifies. Notice, though, that the participle is written beginning on the slanted line and continuing onto the horizontal line. A nominative absolute is diagramed in the same way an expletive is.

PARTICIPIAL PHRASE

Shyly handing the teacher his math paper, Jake asked for help.

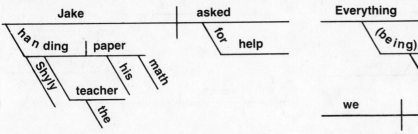

NOMINATIVE ABSOLUTE

Everything finally ready, we relaxed.

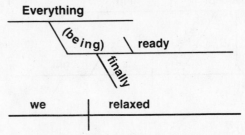

Gerunds and Gerund Phrases

When a gerund is used as a basic sentence part, its pedestal is placed on the base line where that sentence part would normally be. The gerund itself is written on a stepped line, and modifiers and complements, if any, are written in their usual positions. When a gerund is used as an indirect object or object of a preposition it is placed on a stepped line below the main line.

GERUND PHRASE

Our losing the game was a shock.

AS AN INDIRECT OBJECT

Pam gave *writing* all her energy.

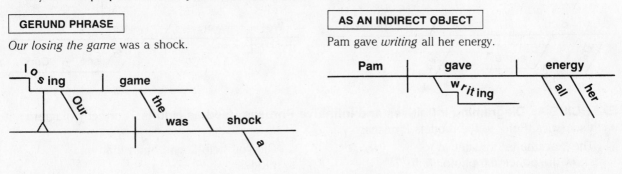

EXERCISE A: Diagraming Participial Phrases and Nominative Absolutes. Correctly diagram each sentence.

1. We approached the table heaped with food.

2. Our spirits confident, we entered the contest.

EXERCISE B: Diagraming Gerunds and Gerund Phrases. Correctly diagram each sentence.

1. We were disturbed by the wailing of the sirens.

2. Jack's hobby, whittling, became his second career.

6.6 Diagraming Phrases

Infinitives and Infinitive Phrases

An infinitive or infinitive phrase used as a noun is diagramed on a pedestal in any of the positions a noun or pronoun would occupy. Subjects, complements, or modifiers of the infinitive—if any—occupy normal positions. Notice how an omitted *to* is handled.

INFINITIVE PHRASE	WITH A SUBJECT

To accept help gracefully is a gift.   We watched *Tony run in the marathon.*

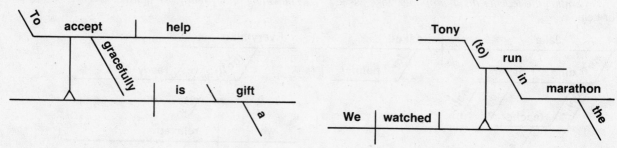

An infinitive or infinitive phrase used as an adjective or an adverb is diagramed in much the same way as a prepositional phrase.

AS AN ADJECTIVE	AS AN ADVERB

The best dish *to serve* is also inexpensive.   We were eager *to see Cary.*

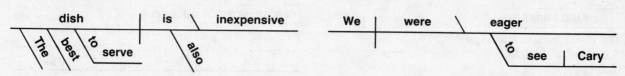

EXERCISE A: Diagraming Infinitives and Infinitive Phrases Used as Nouns. Correctly diagram each sentence. Refer to the models if necessary.

1. The blackmailer threatened to show the police the photographs.

2. Did you help Logan build that model?

EXERCISE B: Diagraming Infinitives and Infinitive Phrases Used as Adjectives and Adverbs. Correctly diagram each sentence.

1. Lucy's suggestion is the one to follow.

2. Few people are happy to work in that factory.

7.1 Adjective Clauses

A clause is a group of words with its own subject and verb. An independent clause can stand by itself as a complete sentence. A subordinate clause can only be part of a sentence.

The Adjective Clause

An adjective clause is a subordinate clause that modifies a noun or pronoun by telling what kind or which one. Adjective clauses begin with relative pronouns or relative adverbs.

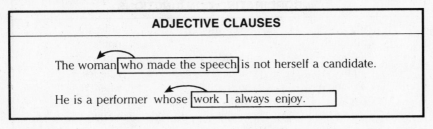

ADJECTIVE CLAUSES
The woman who made the speech is not herself a candidate.
He is a performer whose work I always enjoy.

Introductory Words

Relative pronouns connect adjective clauses to the words they modify. They also play a role within their own clauses, as shown in the chart. Relative adverbs connect adjective clauses to the words they modify and act as adverbs within the clauses. Note in the second example that an introductory word may be understood.

USES OF INTRODUCTORY WORDS
The movie *that is playing now* is a comedy.   (subject)
The movie *(that) we saw last night* was a documentary.   (direct object)
The movie *in which Tony appeared* was a hit.   (object of a preposition)
He is an actor *whose work I admire.*   (adjective)
I remember the day *when they began filming.*   (adverb)

EXERCISE A: Recognizing Adjective Clauses. Underline the adjective clause in each sentence. Circle the word it modifies.

EXAMPLE: Grace is the (person) I met at Reggie's party. _____

1. The house where John F. Kennedy was born is now a museum.

   _____

2. This soup has a spice that I can't identify. _____

3. Mom is the one for whom I left the message. _____

4. Len is the one whose mother is the district attorney. _____

5. Ohio is a state that cherishes football. _____

6. Mr. Paulson is the teacher who inspired me to study chemistry.

   _____

7. Wendy is someone I have known since kindergarten. _____

8. Emily Dickinson is a poet whose work was once ignored. _____

9. A calculator is something Dad will surely like. _____

10. Where is the box in which I keep my change? _____

EXERCISE B: Recognizing the Use of Introductory Words. On the line at the right of each sentence above, write the introductory word and its use in the clause.

EXAMPLE: Grace is the (person) I met at Reggie's party.   _(that)   direct object_

7.2 Adverb Clauses

The Adverb Clause

Subordinate adverb clauses modify verbs, adjectives, adverbs, or verbals by telling where, when, in what manner, to what extent, under what condition, or why. All adverb clauses begin with subordinating conjunctions.

SUBORDINATING CONJUNCTIONS		
after	even though	unless
although	if	until
as	in order that	when
as if	since	whenever
as long as	so that	where
because	than	wherever
before	though	while

ADVERB CLAUSES
When friends sleep over, we don't usually sleep very much.
Anita looks better *than I have ever seen her look before*.
Moving *wherever there was work*, the migrant family had no permanent home.

Elliptical Adverb Clauses

An elliptical clause is one in which the verb or subject and verb are understood but not actually stated.

ELLIPTICAL ADVERB CLAUSES
Verb Understood: Peter was in a bigger hurry *than I* [*was*].
Subject and Verb Understood: I like apple pie better *than* [*I like*] *peach*.

EXERCISE A: Identifying Adverb Clauses. Underline the adverb clause in each sentence. Then circle the subordinating conjunction in each.

EXAMPLE: We enjoyed the picnic (until) the storm began.

1. My parents will be happy if we are home by eleven.
2. We planted the garden where it would get the most sun.
3. Dad volunteers at the hospital whenever he has time.
4. After the butter has melted, add the chopped vegetables.
5. Sally will help if you ask her.

EXERCISE B: Identifying Elliptical Clauses. Underline the adverb clause in each sentence. If the clause is elliptical, write *elliptical* in the space provided. If it is not elliptical, leave the space blank.

EXAMPLE: Is everyone as excited <u>as you</u>? ___*elliptical*___

1. While sick, Fran read several books a day. _____
2. Each applicant was better qualified than the one before. _____
3. Dan is the same age as Ben. _____
4. The couch was delivered today, as the clerk had promised. _____
5. I like swimming better than jogging. _____

7.3 Noun Clauses

The Noun Clause

A noun clause is a subordinate clause that acts as a noun. In a sentence a noun clause may have any function of a single-word noun.

NOUN CLAUSES
Subject: How the accident happened remains a mystery.
Direct Object: We couldn't decide *what the best plan would be.*
Indirect Object: Now you can tell *whomever you want* the plan.
Predicate Nominative: More shelf space is *what you need.*
Object of a Preposition: The committee disagreed about *what its role should be.*
Appositive: His idea, *that all people are equal,* is central to American democracy.

Introductory Words

Introductory words may act as subjects, direct objects, objects of prepositions, adjectives, or adverbs in noun clauses; or they may simply introduce the clauses without any internal function.

USES OF INTRODUCTORY WORDS IN NOUN CLAUSES
Subject: We will nominate whoever can win.
Direct Object: Whomever you hire must have excellent references.
Adjective: I don't know which path is the right one.
Adverb: The usher showed us where we should sit.
No Function: I wonder if you can help me.

EXERCISE A: Identifying Noun Clauses. Underline the noun clause in each sentence. In the first space at the right, tell the function of the clause: *S* (subject), *DO* (direct object), *IO* (indirect object), *PN* (predicate nominative), *OP* (object of a preposition), or *APP* (appositive).

EXAMPLE: We all agreed <u>that you would do a good job</u>. *DO* _____

1. That we arrived just then was lucky. _____ _____

2. Do you know when the last bus leaves? _____ _____

3. The committee will give whoever wins a savings bond. _____ _____

4. That she was sick was obvious to all. _____ _____

5. One consideration was which house has more space. _____ _____

6. I suggest that you enter the contest again. _____ _____

7. We wondered about whatever became of Jane. _____ _____

8. Please tell whomever you see the time of the party. _____ _____

9. What Carol reported surprised all of us. _____ _____

10. Tom's dilemma was whether he should work or go fishing. _____

_____

EXERCISE B: Recognizing the Use of Introductory Words. Write the introductory word from each noun clause above. Then, using the key above plus *ADJ* (adjective), *ADV* (adverb), or *NONE*, write the function of the introductory word within the clause.

EXAMPLE: We all agreed <u>that you would do a good job</u>. *DO*   *that NONE*

7.4 Sentences Classified by Structure and Function

The Four Structures of Sentences

Sentences can be classified by the number and kind of clauses they contain.

Kind of Sentence	Number and Kind of Clauses	Examples (subjects underlined once, verbs twice)
simple	one independent clause (subject or verb or both may be compound)	Tom played well. Tom and Ali played well. Tom and Ali played well and won.
compound	two or more independent clauses	The train arrived on time, but no one got on or off.
complex	one independent clause and one or more subordinate clauses	SUBORD. CLAUSE IND. CLAUSE Though no one got off, we still waited.
compound-complex	two or more independent clauses and one or more subordinate clauses	IND. CLAUSE SUBORD. CLAUSE I saw someone who looked familiar, IND. CLAUSE but it was someone else.

EXERCISE A: Distinguishing Between Simple and Compound Sentences. Identify each sentence as simple or compound. The simple sentences may have compound parts.

EXAMPLE: Kenney swung at the ball and missed.   _simple_

1. We had hoped for a break in the weather, but the forecast is bleak. _____

2. Friends and strangers alike worked side by side piling sandbags. _____

3. Jan poised on the end of the board, took a deep breath, and dived. _____

4. The children may have been pleased, but their parents were not. _____

5. Paul finished his chores early, so he was free to go with us. _____

6. The aide denied ever having made that statement. _____

7. The task seemed impossible; nevertheless, we agreed to try. _____

8. We stood inside the clubhouse, waiting for the rain to stop. _____

9. Some people offered to help; others agreed reluctantly; still others flatly refused. _____

10. Jody made a wish and blew out the candles. _____

EXERCISE B: Identifying the Structure of Sentences. Identify each sentence as (1) simple, (2) compound, (3) complex, or (4) compound-complex by writing the proper number in the blank.

EXAMPLE: Jeremy ordered more than he could eat.   _3_

1. The group is trying to decide how to raise the money. _____

2. The inspector warned the investigators to use extreme caution. _____

3. The horses approached the finish line, and the spectators roared. _____

4. We should hurry, or the train will leave without us. _____

5. The Bombers and the Torpedoes will play in the championship. _____

6. Zoe would be a better choice, for she speaks better than I. _____

7. The President smiled and shook hands with each guest. _____

8. Although I like math and science, I do better in languages. _____

9. The baby picked up the spoon and threw it across the room. _____

10. Can you fix the dessert Hal makes, or shall I have him bring it? _____

7.4 Sentences Classified by Structure and Function

The Four Functions of Sentences

Sentences can also be classified by their function.

Kind of Sentence	Function	Example	End Mark
declarative	states an idea	Those flowers are dandelions.	period (.)
interrogative	asks a question	Where have I seen that face before?	question mark (?)
imperative	gives an order or a direction	Stand still! Fold your paper in half.	period or exclamation mark (. or !)
exclamatory	conveys a strong emotion	What an odd creature that is! How hard we worked!	exclamation mark (!)

EXERCISE A: Identifying the Function of Sentences. Identify each sentence as *declarative, interrogative, imperative,* or *exclamatory*.

EXAMPLE: Leave a message if no one is home. ___*imperative*___

1. Print clearly or type all information needed. _____

2. Have you found the book you were looking for? _____

3. Which of the candidates do you plan to support? _____

4. Trivia games are becoming increasingly popular. _____

5. Be sure the two surfaces are securely glued together. _____

6. What an unkind thing that was to say! _____

7. Follow Main Street for two miles. _____

8. Seashells were an early form of money. _____

9. Smoke curled from the chimney of the little cabin. _____

10. Have you spoken to Megan this week? _____

EXERCISE B: Choosing the Correct End Mark by Function. Supply the correct end mark for each sentence.

EXAMPLE: Chameleons have protective coloration___.___

1. Stop that car_____

2. Did you take a message_____

3. What an unusual shade of red that is_____

4. Drop that gun_____

5. Tomorrow's forecast sounds promising_____

6. Who directed that movie_____

7. Now that's what I call a car_____

8. Deciduous trees shed their leaves in the fall_____

9. Be sure to tell Sandy I stopped by_____

10. Interest on those accounts is compounded daily_____

7.5 Diagraming Clauses

Compound Sentences

Diagram each independent clause of a compound sentence separately. Then join the verbs with a dotted, stepped line, writing the conjunction or semicolon on the dotted line as shown.

INDEPENDENT CLAUSE		INDEPENDENT CLAUSE

I am eager to read Irene's new book, for *her earlier ones were excellent.*

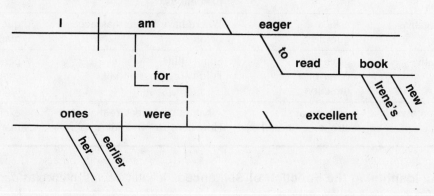

EXERCISE A: Diagraming Compound Sentences. Diagram each sentence correctly. Refer to the model above if you need to.

1. Tie the rope securely, or the swing may fall down.

2. Mike advertised the job widely, but no one applied for it.

EXERCISE B: Diagraming Compound Elements and Compound Sentences. Decide whether each sentence below is a compound sentence or a simple sentence with compound elements. Then diagram each one correctly.

1. Maureen must take the test again or lose credit for the course.

2. Watch your step, for the sidewalk may be slippery.

7.5 | Diagraming Clauses

Complex Sentences

Both adjective and adverb clauses are diagramed on a line beneath the independent clause and connected to the independent clause by a dotted line. With an adjective clause, the dotted line extends from the noun or pronoun the clause modifies to the relative pronoun or relative adverb in the clause.

ADJECTIVE CLAUSES

The boy *that we met* was a friend of yours.

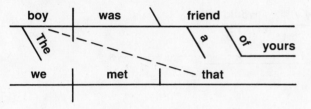

This is a time *when we must act*.

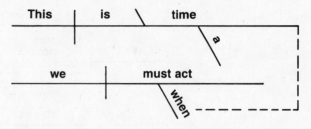

With an adverb clause, the dotted line extends from the word modified to the verb in the adverb clause. The subordinating conjunction is written along the dotted line.

ADVERB CLAUSE

Today I feel more relaxed *than ever*.

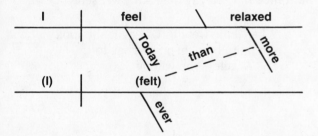

A noun clause is placed on a pedestal extending upward from the position it fills in the sentence. If the introductory word has no function in the sentence, it is written along the pedestal.

NOUN CLAUSE

We wondered *if Al would come*.

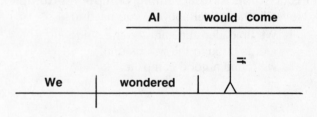

EXERCISE A: Diagraming Adjective and Adverb Clauses. Correctly diagram each sentence.

1. Although you hate the gift, you should write a thank-you note.

2. Edna prepared for the day when she would have her own job.

EXERCISE B: Diagraming Noun Clauses. Correctly diagram each sentence.

1. We promised Mr. Hillyer that we would mow his lawn today.

2. Whatever we decide is likely to displease someone.

7.5 | Diagraming Clauses

Compound-Complex Sentences

When diagraming a compound-complex sentence, begin by diagraming each of the independent clauses. Then diagram the subordinate clause(s).

NOUN CLAUSE		ADVERB CLAUSE

We hoped *that Sandy would join us,* but she stayed home *because she had a cold.*

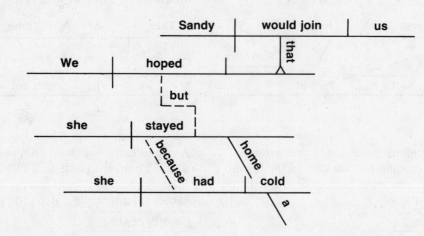

EXERCISE A: Diagraming Compound-Complex Sentences. Correctly diagram each sentence. Refer to the model above if you need to.

1. We unloaded the car, and the guide led us through the woods until we found a good campsite.

2. When Julie went to Chicago, she took the train, but when she goes to Los Angeles, she will fly.

EXERCISE B: Diagraming Sentences of Varying Structures. Identify the structure of each sentence and diagram it correctly.

1. The doctor who made the initial diagnosis has recommended a second opinion.

2. I do not know where you got your information, but I do know that it is inaccurate.

8.1 Fragments and Run-ons

Fragments

Do not capitalize and punctuate phrases, subordinate clauses, or words in a series as if they were complete sentences.

Fragments	Sentences
Without even knocking.	I opened the door without even knocking.
A woman of strong convictions.	We chose Marian, a woman of strong convictions.
Thought long and hard.	Ken thought long and hard before deciding.
A dog, two cats, and a gerbil.	I have a dog, two cats, and a gerbil.
That everyone wants.	The game that everyone wants is on sale.
Where the weather is warmer.	I want to go where the weather is warmer.

EXERCISE A: Identifying Sentence Fragments. Write whether each group of words is a sentence or a fragment.

EXAMPLE: Following her own instincts.   _fragment_

1. To believe everything you hear. _____

2. A person who has everything. _____

3. Who got the right answer? _____

4. The woman on the speaker's platform. _____

5. Plays with enthusiasm and energy. _____

6. Remember the Alamo! _____

7. Heaping platters and bowls of delicacies. _____

8. One of the most exciting performances I have ever seen. _____

9. Driving along the Pacific Coast. _____

10. Andrew lost his first tooth. _____

EXERCISE B: Correcting Sentence Fragments. Use five of the fragments you identified in Exercise A in complete sentences.

EXAMPLE: _Following her own instincts often got Clara into trouble._

1. _____

   _____

2. _____

   _____

3. _____

   _____

4. _____

   _____

5. _____

   _____

8.1 Fragments and Run-ons

Run-ons

Use punctuation, conjunctions, or other means to join or separate the parts of a run-on sentence.

Run-on Sentences	Corrected Sentences
The dog ran away no one ever found it.	The dog ran away; no one ever found it. The dog ran away, and no one ever found it. The dog ran away and was never found.
Ella found the treasure, she never told anyone.	Ella found the treasure. She never told anyone. Ella found the treasure but never told anyone. Although Ella found the treasure, she never told anyone.

EXERCISE A: Identifying Run-ons. Label each item below as a run-on or a sentence.

EXAMPLE: The fans were eager for a win the odds were against it.   _run-on_

1. Gloria offered to make baked Alaska, which is her specialty. _____

2. The beach is pleasant during the week, it is crowded on weekends. _____

3. The play was excellent, the cast was only mediocre. _____

4. Jason wants to become a teacher, he is my brother. _____

5. Wringing her hands nervously, Alicia paced back and forth in her dressing room.

   _____

6. You'll love that book it's a mystery. _____

7. Ben applied for a variety of jobs, everyone said he was over qualified. _____

8. In general I hate exercise swimming is one thing I do enjoy. _____

9. Juliette fell off the swing, she broke her wrist. _____

10. Whenever we visit our cousins, we either take a picnic to the park or spend the day at the beach.

   _____

EXERCISE B: Correcting Run-ons. Correct five of the run-ons you identified in Exercise A, using a variety of methods.

EXAMPLE: _Although the fans were eager for a win, the odds were against it._

1. _____
   _____

2. _____
   _____

3. _____
   _____

4. _____
   _____

5. _____
   _____

8.2 | Misplaced and Dangling Modifiers

Recognizing Misplaced and Dangling Modifiers

A modifier should be placed as close as possible to the word it modifies. A misplaced modifier appears to modify the wrong word in a sentence. A dangling modifier appears to modify the wrong word or no word at all because the word it should logically modify is missing.

Misplaced Modifier	Dangling Modifier
Jack got a watch from his uncle *with fluorescent hands*.	*Sniffing the carton cautiously,* the milk didn't smell sour.

EXERCISE A: Recognizing Misplaced Modifiers. Underline each misplaced modifier. If a sentence contains no misplaced modifier, leave it unmarked.

EXAMPLE: Dr. Sweet showed pictures of rare birds he had photographed <u>at the Rotary Club</u>.

1. Nancy discovered that Bowser had eaten the tea sandwiches with a cry of dismay.
2. His mother had asked Charles to have his hair cut a dozen times.
3. Stepping off the curb, Aunt Clare was nearly hit by a delivery truck.
4. Merriwell vowed to set a new freestyle record with deep emotion in his voice.
5. Erin was reading limericks written by Edward Lear with squeals of delight.
6. Written in Portuguese, the message made no sense to Arthur.
7. Dad called to me to finish mowing the lawn from the upstairs window.
8. Maggie found a sweater that had never been worn in the thrift shop.
9. John was reprimanded for his classroom behavior in the principal's office.
10. Dad bought a desk from an antique dealer with a secret compartment.

EXERCISE B: Recognizing Dangling Modifiers. Underline each dangling modifier. If a sentence contains no dangling modifier, leave it unmarked.

EXAMPLE: <u>Before handing in your paper</u>, each answer should be carefully checked.

1. Flying low over the treetops, a herd of elephants charged into our view.
2. Shucking oysters at Caro's Clam Bar, a huge pearl was discovered.
3. Marking the way with string, Theseus was able to find his way back out of the maze.
4. Clearing the bar at seventeen feet, a new record was set.
5. The ball was lost practicing last week.
6. How beautiful the autumn foliage looked motoring through Vermont!
7. Cheered by a taste of success, his next play had a happy ending.
8. Checking through her calculation, Mary found her error and corrected it.
9. Peering through the keyhole, nothing in the room seemed out of order.
10. Arriving at the theater an hour late, the seats were taken.

8.2 | Misplaced and Dangling Modifiers

Correcting Misplaced Modifiers

Correct a misplaced modifier by moving the phrase or clause closer to the word it should logically modify.

Misplaced Modifiers	Corrected Sentences
Clara saw the tornado approaching *through the bedroom window*.	Through the bedroom window, Clara saw the tornado approaching.
Hugo wore a hat on his head *that was several sizes too small*.	Hugo wore a hat that was several sizes too small on his head. On his head, Hugo wore a hat that was several sizes too small.

EXERCISE A: Recognizing Misplaced Modifiers. Underline each misplaced modifier.

EXAMPLE: I was happy to find the cookies in my lunchbox <u>that my mother made</u>.

1. Tonight, WCTV presents a special program for viewers interested in changing to new careers at 8:00 P.M.
2. The retriever swam to his master on shore with a duck in his mouth.
3. Dad took the picture of the white-billed noddy using his high-speed camera.
4. The customer demanded an explanation in an angry voice.
5. Cheering wildly, the home team was greeted by their fans.
6. Mom remembered she had not turned the oven off in the middle of our trip.
7. Please don't give scraps to the dogs with small bones in them.
8. We saw many fine old houses strolling around the village green.
9. David waited patiently for a bee to come along with a jelly jar.
10. Let us know if you plan to make the trip on the enclosed postcard.

EXERCISE B: Correcting Misplaced Modifiers. Rewrite five sentences in Exercise A, correcting the misplaced modifiers.

EXAMPLE: _I was happy to find in my lunchbox the cookies that my mother made._

1. _____
   _____
2. _____
   _____
3. _____
   _____
4. _____
   _____
5. _____
   _____

8.2 | Misplaced and Dangling Modifiers

Correcting Dangling Modifiers

Correct a dangling modifier by rewriting the sentence to include the missing word.

Dangling Modifier	Corrected Sentences
Reaching the top of the hill, the camp was a welcome sight.	Reaching the top of the hill, we found the camp a welcome sight. When we reached the top of the hill, the camp was a welcome sight.

EXERCISE A: Recognizing Dangling Modifiers. Underline each dangling modifier.

EXAMPLE: <u>Waiting in the wings</u>, stage fright gripped her heart.

1. Strolling through the narrow streets, the native quarter was picturesque.
2. Searching for the missing contract, the whole house was turned upside down.
3. Doing my homework, the radio next door was distracting.
4. Before parking in that lot, a sticker must be purchased.
5. His wallet was stolen while watching the fireworks display.
6. Having sent the suspect to jail, the case seemed to be closed.
7. Vegetation became sparse approaching the summit of the mountain.
8. While farming in Texas, oil was discovered.
9. Entering the dining room, the roast turkey looked appetizing.
10. Born into an immigrant family, the White House seemed an impossible goal.

EXERCISE B: Correcting Dangling Modifiers. Rewrite five sentences in Exercise A, correcting the dangling modifiers.

EXAMPLE: _Waiting in the wings, the actress felt stage fright grip her heart._

1. _____
_____
2. _____
_____
3. _____
_____
4. _____
_____
5. _____
_____

8.3 | Faulty Parallelism

Recognizing Faulty Parallelism

Parallelism is the placement of equal ideas in words, phrases, or clauses of similar type.

SOME COMMON PARALLEL STRUCTURES

Parallel Words: The camp has excellent facilities for *riding, hiking,* and *swimming*.

Parallel Phrases: Jennings had gone to the country *to rest, to think,* and *to catch a few fish*.

Parallel Clauses: A news story should tell *what happened, when it happened,* and *who was involved*.

EXERCISE A: Recognizing Parallel Ideas. Underline the parallel ideas in each sentence.

EXAMPLE: Ms. Downing has already gained considerable fame <u>on stage</u>, <u>on television</u>, and <u>in the movies</u>.

1. The summer program includes courses in cooking, sewing, and painting.
2. The safest way to lose weight is by eating less and by exercising more.
3. Entries will be judged for originality and for aptness of expression.
4. The history of the Pony Express was brief but colorful.
5. Polonius advised his son to be true to himself, to value his friends, and to keep his own counsel.
6. The increase in the sales tax will not affect the prices of groceries, children's clothing, or prescription drugs.
7. Management hopes to improve profits by cutting costs, increasing productivity, and improving distribution.
8. Ms. Collins stressed the importance of taking careful notes and reviewing the material daily.
9. As yet the inspector has no idea who could have committed so bizarre a crime or what the motive might have been.
10. A good adviser should be imaginative, patient, and sympathetic.

EXERCISE B: Distinguishing Between Correct and Faulty Parallelism. In the blank at the right, indicate whether each sentence is correct as written (C) or contains faulty parallelism (F).

EXAMPLE: The guidance counselor recommended studying harder and to turn off the television set at homework time. ___F___

1. You can apply the stain with a cloth or by brushing it on. _____
2. The witness testified calmly, clearly, and convincingly. _____
3. A successful ballerina needs skill, stamina, and to have good coordination. _____
4. Skateboarding, roller skating, and bicycle riding are not permitted. _____
5. The inspector reported the situation and that something should be done. _____
6. The morning was hot, muggy, and with a cloudy sky. _____
7. The Ferret is roomy, inexpensive, and operates efficiently. _____
8. Carol likes browsing through encyclopedias and to learn odd facts. _____
9. The company's annual report showed an increase in sales but that profits had dropped. _____
10. Disease-causing agents may be present in air, food, or water. _____

8.3 Faulty Parallelism

Correcting Faulty Parallelism

Correct a sentence containing faulty parallelism by rewriting it so that each parallel idea is expressed in the same grammatical structure.

Nonparallel Structures	Parallel Structures
The manager protested *loudly* and *with emotion*.	The manager protested *loudly* and *emotionally*.
A guard dog must be *tough, obedient,* and *without fear*.	A guard dog must be *tough, obedient,* and *fearless*.
Mr. Darling liked *weeding his garden, mowing his lawn,* and *to putter around his house*.	Mr. Darling liked *weeding his garden, mowing his lawn,* and *puttering around his house*.
The twins were identical *in appearance* and how they behaved.	The twins were identical in *appearance* and *behavior*.
The Dolphins were elated *over defeating the Seals* and *because they had won the championship*.	The Dolphins were elated over *defeating the Seals* and *winning the championship*.

EXERCISE A: Identifying Faulty Parallelism. Underline the nonparallel structures in each sentence below.

EXAMPLE: The children loved <u>playing in the surf</u> and <u>to build sand castles on the beach</u>.

1. The candidate was criticized for being colorless and that he was overly cautious.
2. Paul likes cooking but dislikes to clean up afterward.
3. Mr. Asforis needs someone who will help in the stock room and to make deliveries.
4. Reading the book was fun but to write a report on it was hard.
5. The pianist played with great feeling but occasionally hitting some sour notes.
6. The scouts especially liked hiking and to camp out.
7. The company can become profitable by cutting costs or sell more widgets.
8. Nick enjoyed receiving letters but not to write them.
9. The main duties of the job are typing, filing, and to do simple bookkeeping.
10. If you plan on flying or to take a train this weekend, you can expect crowds.

EXERCISE B: Correcting Faulty Parallelism. Rewrite five sentences in Exercise A, correcting the faulty parallelism.

EXAMPLE: *The children loved to play in the surf and to build sand castles on the beach.*

1. _____
   _____
2. _____
   _____
3. _____
   _____
4. _____
   _____
5. _____
   _____

9.1 The Varieties of English

Standard English

Standard English can be either formal or informal. Formal English uses traditional standards of correctness. It is characterized by elaborate sentence structures and an extensive vocabulary. Informal English is conversational in tone. It uses a smaller vocabulary than formal English and generally shorter sentences.

Formal English	Informal English
His intense scrutiny of the specimen failed to disclose shards of a metallic substance.	When he looked closely at the sample, he didn't see any metal fragments.

Nonstandard English

Nonstandard English includes slang and dialect. A nonstandard dialect is a form of English that makes use of words, pronunciations, and sentence structures not used in standard English. Slang is a nonstandard form of English that is colorful and expressive but short-lived.

Slang	Nonstandard Dialect
Eddy really freaked when the dude he worked for came down on him.	It took a powerful smart sheriff to round up those tough ombres.

EXERCISE A: Distinguishing Among Varieties of English. Label each item below *F* (formal), *I* (informal), *S* (slang), or *D* (dialect).

EXAMPLE: We couldn't help but take a shine to the ol' codger. __*D*__

1. Alvin is a precocious youngster with an extensive lexicon. _____

2. Y'all lemme know if'n y'ave a speck o' trouble. _____

3. Let me help you with that package. _____

4. Old Man Jenkins sure got the shaft in that real estate swindle. _____

5. I'll be finished with this in just a second. _____

6. Those two're closer 'n a tick on a dog's ear. _____

7. Jed's overriding commitment to egalitarian principles prompted his vehement critique of the editorial. _____

8. Y'all gonna git in a mess o' trouble for bad talkin' Miz Jones. _____

9. Are you giving it to me straight or are you jiving me? _____

10. For his age, Jimmy is a pretty good little soccer player. _____

EXERCISE B: Changing Nonstandard English into Standard English. Rewrite five sentences that you labeled *S* or *D* in Exercise A using standard English.

EXAMPLE: _We could not help liking the old gentleman._

1. _____

2. _____

3. _____

4. _____

5. _____

10.1 Verb Tenses

The Six Tenses of Verbs

A tense is a form of a verb that shows the time of action or state of being. Each tense has a basic and a progressive form.

Tenses	Basic Forms	Progressive Forms
Present	He *obeys*.	He *is obeying*.
Past	He *obeyed*.	He *was obeying*.
Future	He *will obey.*	He *will be obeying*.
Present Perfect	He *has obeyed*.	He *has been obeying*.
Past Perfect	He *had obeyed*.	He *had been obeying*.
Future Perfect	He *will have obeyed*.	He *will have been obeying*.

The Four Principal Parts of Verbs

A verb has four principal parts: the present, the present participle, the past, and the past participle.

THE FOUR PRINCIPAL PARTS			
Present	**Present Participle**	**Past**	**Past Participle**
arrive	arriving	arrived	(have) arrived
begin	beginning	began	(have) begun
buy	buying	bought	(have) bought

EXERCISE A: Recognizing Tenses and Forms of Verbs. Underline the verb or verb phrase in each sentence below. Then write the tense on each line to the right. If the form is progressive, write the word *progressive* after the tense.

EXAMPLE: We <u>have been hearing</u> rumors about Jake.   *present perfect progressive*

1. I followed the recipe carefully. _____

2. The state police were pulling over many drivers. _____

3. I have tried several times to lose weight. _____

4. Tomorrow Grandma will have been visiting here a month. _____

5. That shop carries beautiful fabrics. _____

6. Soon that group will release a new video. _____

7. Dad and I will be waiting for you at the station. _____

8. Columbus had planned to reach the Orient. _____

9. Detectives had been investigating for months. _____

10. The workers will have finished by now. _____

EXERCISE B: Identifying Principal Parts. On the lines below, write the principal part used to form the verb in each sentence above. Then write the name of that principal part.

EXAMPLE: *hearing   present participle*

1. _____   6. _____

2. _____   7. _____

3. _____   8. _____

4. _____   9. _____

5. _____   10. _____

10.1 Verb Tenses

Regular and Irregular Verbs

A regular verb is one whose past and past participle are formed by adding -ed or -d to the present form.

PRINCIPAL PARTS OF REGULAR VERBS			
Present	Present Participle	Past	Past Participle
cry	crying	cried	(have) cried
drop	dropping	dropped	(have) dropped
deprive	depriving	deprived	(have) deprived
grant	granting	granted	(have) granted

An irregular verb is one whose past and past participle are not formed by adding -ed or -d to the present form.

PRINCIPAL PARTS OF IRREGULAR VERBS			
Present	Present Participle	Past	Past Participle
hurt	hurting	hurt	(have) hurt
shut	shutting	shut	(have) shut
find	finding	found	(have) found
teach	teaching	taught	(have) taught
fly	flying	flew	(have) flown
sing	singing	sang	(have) sung
write	writing	wrote	(have) written

EXERCISE A: Writing the Principal Parts of Irregular Verbs. Add the missing principal parts.

EXAMPLE: rise _____*rising*_____ _____*rose*_____ _____*(have) risen*_____

1. _____ beginning _____ _____

2. _____ _____ drew _____

3. freeze _____ _____ _____

4. _____ _____ _____ (have) run

5. _____ _____ put _____

6. _____ thinking _____ _____

7. _____ _____ _____ (have) fallen

8. catch _____ _____ _____

9. _____ _____ bound _____

10. _____ speaking _____ _____

EXERCISE B: Recognizing Principal Parts of Verbs. Fill in each blank with the correct verb form from those given in parentheses.

EXAMPLE: The final bell hasn't __*rung*__ yet.   (rang, rung)

1. Our water pipes _____ during the January freeze.   (burst, busted)

2. We _____ the blanket on the sand.   (spread, spreaded)

3. Paula _____ her foil at her opponent's vest.   (thrust, thrusted)

4. Brenda has _____ in competitions for years.   (dived, dove)

5. Someone has _____ into the computer file.   (broke, broken)

10.1 Verb Tenses

Conjugating the Tenses

A conjugation is a complete list of the singular and plural forms of a verb. A short conjugation lists just the forms that are used with a single pronoun. As you study the following short conjugations, note that the verbs used with *you* are also used with *we* and *they*. The verbs used with *she*, likewise, are also used with *he* and *it*.

SHORT CONJUGATIONS			
Basic, Progressive, and Emphatic Forms	**go (with *I*)**	**go (with *you*)**	**go (with *she*)**
Present	I go	you go	she goes
Past	I went	you went	she went
Future	I will go	you will go	she will go
Present Perfect	I have gone	you have gone	she has gone
Past Perfect	I had gone	you had gone	she had gone
Future Perfect	I will have gone	you will have gone	she will have gone
Present Progressive	I am going	you are going	she is going
Past Progressive	I was going	you were going	she was going
Future Progressive	I will be going	you will be going	she will be going
Present Perfect Progressive	I have been going	you have been going	she has been going
Past Perfect Progressive	I had been going	you had been going	she had been going
Future Perfect Progressive	I will have been going	you will have been going	she will have been going
Present Emphatic	I do go	you do go	she does go
Past Emphatic	I did go	you did go	she did go

EXERCISE A: Conjugating Verbs. Complete each of the following short conjugations, giving all six basic forms and the first three progressive forms.

1. try (with *I*)   2. find (with *he*)   3. speak (with *we*)   4. run (with *they*)

_____   _____   _____   _____

_____   _____   _____   _____

_____   _____   _____   _____

_____   _____   _____   _____

_____   _____   _____   _____

_____   _____   _____   _____

_____   _____   _____   _____

_____   _____   _____   _____

_____   _____   _____   _____

EXERCISE B: Supplying the Correct Verb Form. Fill in each blank with the form of each verb given in parentheses.

EXAMPLE: I ___*will be studying*___ French next year. (*study*, future progressive)

1. We _____ our theory in the lab. (*test*, future perfect)

2. The lake _____ during the first week in January. (*freeze*, past)

3. Dad _____ the mantel clock already. (*wind*, present perfect)

4. Uncle Ed _____ dinner on Friday. (*prepare*, past emphatic)

5. The candidate _____ lower taxes. (*promise*, past perfect)

10.2 Expressing Time Through Tense

Uses of Tense in Present Time

The three forms of the present tense show present actions or conditions as well as various continuous actions or conditions.

USES OF TENSE IN PRESENT TIME		
Verb Forms	**Uses**	**Examples**
Present	Present action Present condition	There *goes* the balloon. The band *sounds* wonderful.
	Recurring action Recurring condition	I *pack* my own lunch. The paramedics *are* prompt to arrive.
	Constant action Constant condition	The earth *rotates* on its axis. Pluto *is* the most distant planet.
Present Progressive	Continuing action Continuing condition	I *am studying* for a math test. Lenny *is being* stubborn today.
Present Emphatic	Emphasizing a statement Denying an assertion	I *do hope* for sun this weekend. Despite the rumors, we *do have* school tomorrow.

EXERCISE A: Identifying the Uses of Tense in Present Time. Identify the use of the verb in each sentence, using the labels in the chart above.

EXAMPLE: Paul practices the piano before school every day. ___*recurring action*___

1. Jim certainly does study hard. _____

2. The Mississippi River begins in Minnesota. _____

3. Kyle mows the lawn during summer vacation. _____

4. All of these dishes taste alike tonight. _____

5. I hear a noise in the basement. _____

6. Grandpa is taking a nap. _____

7. A perpetual flame burns in Arlington Cemetery. _____

8. Regardless of earlier reports, Ed does plan to enter the race. _____

9. Mom commutes sixty miles every day. _____

10. My brother is going to school in Ohio now. _____

EXERCISE B: Using Present Tense Forms in Sentences. Complete each sentence by filling in an appropriate verb form showing present time.

EXAMPLE: Terri ___*walks*___ two miles every morning.

1. Sid _____ the cows now, but he will finish soon.

2. Although she is new in town, Beth _____ quite a few friends.

3. Our neighbors _____ to Alaska.

4. These sweet rolls _____ delicious.

5. Uncle Jack always _____ a nap after lunch.

6. I _____ *The Wind in the Willows* to my younger brother.

7. In spite of its high prices, the shop _____ many customers.

8. A hurricane _____ off the Florida coast.

9. Some people _____ to see you now.

10. Dan _____ German.

10.2 Expressing Time Through Tense

Uses of Tense in Past Time

The seven forms that express past time show actions and conditions beginning in the past.

USES OF TENSES IN PAST TIME		
Verb Forms	**Uses**	**Examples**
Past	Indefinite past time Definite past time	Jake *mowed* the lawn. Tim *was* sick yesterday.
Present Perfect	Indefinite past time Continuing to present	Janet *has finished* her paper. Grandma *has been* busy all day.
Past Perfect	Completed before another past event	The caller *had hung* up by the the time I got to the phone.
Past Progressive	Continuous past event	The sun *was shining* yesterday.
Present Perfect Progressive	Event continuing to present	I *have been studying* all weekend.
Past Perfect Progressive	Continuous past event before another	Before the storm, we *had been enjoying* our picnic.
Past Emphatic	Emphasizing a statement Denying an assertion	I *did finish* in time. Despite Brenda's account, Ali *did complete* the event.

EXERCISE A: Identifying the Uses of Tenses in Past Time. Identify the use of the verb in each sentence, using the labels in the chart above.

EXAMPLE: The cast has been rehearsing for a month.   *event continuing to present*

1. Before the opening, the producers had hoped for a hit. _____

2. Bruno was sleeping on the front porch. _____

3. Doris baby-sat for the Holmans. _____

4. We have visited Niagara Falls. _____

5. Several patients were angry about the long wait. _____

EXERCISE B: Using Tenses in Past Time. Write the correct form of the verb in parentheses.

EXAMPLE: The host __*served*__ a fine meal last night.   (served, has been serving)

1. I _____ my homework and crawled into bed.   (was finishing, had finished)

2. Bernie _____ my best friend since kindergarten.   (has been, was being)

3. When we got to the station, the train _____.   (has left, had left)

4. The new play _____ last night.   (opened, has opened)

5. When I met Lydia, she _____ in a fabric store.   (has worked, was working)

6. Andrea protested that she _____ the present.   (was liking, did like)

7. The candidate _____ signatures on the petition since dawn.   (has been gathering, gathered)

8. Cori _____ for the job yesterday.   (applied, has applied)

9. I _____ for the bus when Kim came by.   (waited, was waiting)

10.2 Expressing Time Through Tense

Uses of Tense in Future Time

The four forms that express future time show future actions or conditions.

USES OF TENSES IN FUTURE TIME		
Verb Forms	**Uses**	**Examples**
Future	Future event	Grandma *will visit* us next week.
Future Perfect	Future event before another future event	We *will have finished* our chores before lunch.
Future Progressive	Continuing future event	The scouts *will be selling* cookies all of next month.
Future Perfect Progressive	Continuing future event before another	By opening night, the actors *will have been rehearsing* for six weeks.

EXERCISE A: Identifying the Uses of Tenses in Future Time. Identify the use of the verb in each sentence, using the labels in the chart above.

EXAMPLE: The weather tomorrow will be perfect.   *future event*

1. The circus will be coming to town next week. _____

2. The roofers will have delivered the shingles by noon. _____

3. The stores will be starting their white sales next week. _____

4. The whole family will go out for dinner. _____

5. Soon we will have been waiting here for an hour. _____

6. A new catalog will be arriving shortly. _____

7. Jason will have completed his research by then. _____

8. Next year, Ali will have been performing for a decade. _____

9. Jodi will be visiting several colleges next weekend. _____

10. By dinner time, the gelatin will have set. _____

EXERCISE B: Using Tenses in Future Time. Fill in each blank with the indicated form of the verb in parentheses.

EXAMPLE: The President   *will address*   Congress tonight.   (*address,* future)

1. A local restaurant _____ the party.   (*cater,* future progressive)

2. A real disc jockey _____ records.   (*play,* future progressive)

3. By midnight, they _____ on the flagpole for seventeen hours.   (*sit,* future perfect progressive)

4. The shipment you ordered _____ soon.   (*arrive,* future progressive)

5. Surely you _____ Tanya to the party.   (*invite,* future)

6. Before the play, we _____ the town with posters.   (*paper,* future perfect)

7. This term, I _____ six credits.   (*take,* future progressive)

8. By the time we get there, all the singers _____.   (*perform,* future perfect)

9. The team _____ its first game on Saturday.   (*play,* future progressive)

10. Mom _____ your call when she gets back.   (*return,* future)

10.2 Expressing Time Through Tense

Shifts in Tense

When showing a sequence of events, do not shift tenses unnecessarily.

Unnecessary (Incorrect) Shifts	Correct Sequence
I *had promised* to help Sylvia, but I *forget*.	I *had promised* to help Sylvia, but I *forgot*.
Our cat *has* its own basket. The dog *slept* on my bed.	The cat *has* its own basket. The dog *sleeps* on my bed.
If you *look* carefully, you *saw* the brush strokes.	If you *look* carefully, you *will see* the brush strokes.

Modifiers That Help Clarify Tense

Use modifiers to help clarify the time expressed by a verb.

MODIFIERS EXPRESSING TIME
I *often* study in the library.
That rock group has become very popular *recently*.
Someone will install the telephone *before noon*.

EXERCISE A: Recognizing and Correcting Unnecessary Shifts in Tense. Rewrite each sentence below that has an unnecessary shift in tense. If a sentence is correct as written, write *correct* on the line.

EXAMPLE: I will drive you to school if you needed a ride.
<u>*I will drive you to school if you need a ride.*</u>

1. We never watch television until we finished our homework.

   _____

2. My brother will study law when he will graduate from college.

   _____

3. Phil started jogging before he warms up.

   _____

4. We found the library book right where we were leaving it.

   _____

5. I will have finished my report long before it is due.

   _____

EXERCISE B: Using Modifiers to Help Clarify Tense. Fill in each blank with a modifier that helps to make clear the tense of the sentence.

EXAMPLE: <u>*Late last night*</u>   I heard a strange sound in the attic.

1. I will return your book before you go on vacation _____.
2. The baby has been cranky _____ because she missed her nap.
3. _____, Laura became an outstanding gymnast.
4. When we got to the gate, the plane had _____ left.
5. I will be there _____ to watch you play.

10.3 Active and Passive Voice

Differences Between Active and Passive Verbs

Voice is the form of a verb that shows whether or not the subject is performing the action. A verb is active if its subject performs the action. A verb is passive if its action is performed upon the subject.

Active Voice	Passive Voice
Uncle Lou *met* our plane.	Our plane *was met* by Uncle Lou.
My aunt *taught* me to play the piano.	I *was taught* to play the piano by my aunt.

The Forms of Passive Verbs

A passive verb is made from a form of *be* plus the past participle of a transitive verb.

THE VERB *CATCH* IN THE PASSIVE VOICE		
Tense	Basic Forms	Progressive Forms
Present	I am caught	I am being caught
Past	I was caught	I was being caught
Future	I will be caught	
Present Perfect	I have been caught	
Past Perfect	I had been caught	
Future Perfect	I will have been caught	

EXERCISE A: Distinguishing Between the Active and Passive Voice. After each sentence, write *active* or *passive* to describe the verb.

EXAMPLE: The test flight was made over the desert. ___*passive*___

1. The ambulance has been called. _____

2. This bread was baked by my grandmother. _____

3. The doctor warned against using too much salt. _____

4. A new slate of officers has been nominated. _____

5. The movie was reviewed favorably by several critics. _____

6. The manufacturer will advertise the new product heavily. _____

7. A new strain of bacteria has been identified. _____

8. I have been having trouble concentrating today. _____

9. Despite her years of training, Michelle has never performed publicly. _____

10. Several city officials have been asked to resign. _____

EXERCISE B: Forming Tenses of Passive Verbs. Write the basic forms of each of the following verbs in the passive voice.

1. find (with *you*)	2. make (with *it*)	3. see (with *he*)	4. like (with *they*)
_____	_____	_____	_____
_____	_____	_____	_____
_____	_____	_____	_____
_____	_____	_____	_____
_____	_____	_____	_____
_____	_____	_____	_____

10.3 Active and Passive Voice

Using Voice Correctly

Use the active voice whenever possible. Use the passive voice to emphasize the receiver of an action rather than the performer of an action. Also use the passive voice to point out the receiver of an action whenever the performer is not important or not easily identified.

VERBS IN THE PASSIVE VOICE	
Unnecessary Passive	**Appropriate Passive**
Our table *was served* first by the waiter.	The President's speech *will be carried* by all the networks. The visiting dignitaries *were seated* in the royal box.

EXERCISE A: Distinguishing Between Appropriate and Unnecessary Uses of Passive Voice. Label the three appropriate uses of the passive in the following sentences *A*. Label the other sentences *U*.

EXAMPLE: We were kept after school by the principal. ___*U*___

1. A roar was given by the crowd. _____

2. The actor was acclaimed for his performance. _____

3. Many of the ornaments were made by my grandmother. _____

4. The blue ribbon was won by a friend of mine. _____

5. That new store will be closed on Saturdays. _____

6. Tonight dinner was cooked by Dad. _____

7. All contest entries must be mailed by December 31. _____

8. Winners will be notified by the judges. _____

9. The report is being investigated by the police. _____

10. The arrival of the British troops was announced by Paul Revere. _____

EXERCISE B: Using the Active Voice. Rewrite five of the sentences that you labeled *U* in Exercise A. Change or add words as necessary to put each verb into the active voice.

EXAMPLE: *The principal kept us after school.*

1. _____

2. _____

3. _____

4. _____

5. _____

11.1 The Cases of Pronouns

The Three Cases

Case is the form of a noun or a pronoun that indicates its use in a sentence. The three cases are the nominative, the objective, and the possessive.

CASE FORMS OF PRONOUNS		
Case	Use in Sentence	Forms
Nominative	subject, predicate nominative	I; you; he, she, it; we; they
Objective	direct object, indirect object, object of preposition	me; you; him, her, it; us; them
Possessive	to show ownership	my, mine; your, yours; his; her, hers; its; our, ours; their, theirs

EXERCISE A: Identifying Case. Write the case of each underlined pronoun.

EXAMPLE: Before vigorous exercise, <u>we</u> always warm up. ___*nominative*___

1. Did the usher give <u>you</u> a program? _____
2. Thomas has lent me <u>his</u> history notes. _____
3. Mandy is bringing <u>her</u> famous brownies to the party. _____
4. Do all of these cookies have nuts in <u>them</u>? _____
5. The book on the table is <u>yours</u>. _____
6. A movie that <u>I</u> want to see is playing at the Bijou. _____
7. The doctor is redecorating <u>her</u> office. _____
8. Ben said that you told <u>him</u> about the party. _____
9. The cat curled up in <u>its</u> basket. _____
10. Uncle Jim lent <u>us</u> his projector. _____

EXERCISE B: Identifying Pronoun Case and Use. Write the case of each underlined pronoun. Then write the abbreviation that describes how the pronoun is used in the sentence: *S* (subject), *PN* (predicate nominative), *DO* (direct object), *IO* (indirect object), *OP* (object of a preposition), *O* (to show ownership).

EXAMPLE: The strongest candidates are Beth and <u>you</u>. ___*nominative*   *PN*___

1. Ms. Emmons showed <u>us</u> a new glazing technique. _____
2. Peter and <u>he</u> rotate at first base. _____
3. Did I get a call from Donna or <u>him</u>? _____
4. Each book should have a code number on <u>its</u> spine. _____
5. <u>They</u> ordered the car in plenty of time. _____
6. We felt bad because no one invited <u>us</u>. _____
7. Alicia practiced <u>her</u> piece for the recital. _____
8. The new hall monitors are Harry and <u>I</u>. _____
9. My grandparents have offered us <u>their</u> summer cottage. _____
10. Jason will be spending the weekend with <u>us</u>. _____

11.1 The Cases of Pronouns

The Nominative Case

Use the nominative case for the subject of a verb or for a predicate nominative. When a pronoun used as a subject or predicate nominative is followed by an appostive, the nominative case is still used.

USES OF NOMINATIVE CASE	
Subject	Janet and *she* are sharing an apartment. *We* players pay for our own uniforms.
Predicate Nominative	I think the caller was *she*. The first team up is *we* Sockers.

The Objective Case

Use the objective case for the object of any verb, preposition, or verbal.

USES OF OBJECTIVE CASE	
Direct Object	The course will train *us* in CPR. Dad drove Jed and *me* to the fire station. They announced *us* gymnasts one by one.
Indirect Object	The judges awarded *her* a blue ribbon. Mom ordered Sue and *me* new shoes. The guide showed *us* tourists the White House.
Object of a Preposition	I mailed an invitation to *him* yesterday. You may leave the package with Dan or *me*. The announcer seemed to speak directly to *us* viewers.
Object of a Verbal	Encouraging *us*, she waved from the sidelines. Mr. Koch liked eating tomatoes but not growing *them*. Molly considered the new book and decided to give *it* a try.

EXERCISE A: Identifying Pronouns in the Nominative Case. Circle the nominative pronoun form in parentheses. Then write *S* (subject) or *PN* (predicate nominative) to describe its use.

EXAMPLE: Vivian and (he) him) ordered the shore dinner. __*S*__

1. Hal and (I, me) help with many household chores. _____
2. The new student in our homeroom is (he, him). _____
3. The most likely suspects are (they, them). _____
4. (Her, She) offered a large reward for the return of the lost dog. _____
5. Dave or (he, him) can give you directions. _____

EXERCISE B: Identifying Pronouns in the Objective Case. Circle the objective pronoun form in parentheses. Then write *DO* (direct object), *IO* (indirect object), or *OP* (objective of a preposition) to describe its use.

EXAMPLE: Mme. Karla showed (us) we) dancers a new step. __*IO*__

1. Jenny told (her, she). _____
2. Jo bought this for (he, him). _____
3. Give (we, us) kids a chance. _____
4. Lend (I, me) a hand. _____
5. Are these for Harry or (I, me)? _____
6. I told (them, they) the news. _____
7. Show this to (she, her). _____
8. I have never met (him, he). _____
9. Did you see (us, we)? _____
10. The fans gave (us, we) players a cheer. _____

11.1 The Cases of Pronouns

The Possessive Case

Use the possessive case before nouns and before gerunds to show ownership. Use certain possessive pronouns by themselves to indicate possession.

USES OF THE POSSESSIVE CASE	
Before Nouns	Have you found *your* keys? Jared has not chosen *his* courses yet.
Before Gerunds	All of the other students admired *her* writing. *His* whining annoyed all of us.
Alone	The sweater on the yard chair is *hers,* not *his.* Is that desk *yours* or *mine?*

EXERCISE A: Using Pronouns in the Possessive Case. Choose the correct word in each set of parentheses to complete the sentences below.

EXAMPLE: Please put the record back into ___*its*___ jacket.   (it's, its)

1. _____ working at night has changed the family's schedule.   (Him, His)

2. That statue of a woman on a horse is _____.   (mine, my)

3. Mrs. Killian complimented _____ handling of the incident.   (our, us)

4. I brought my towel along, but I couldn't find _____.   (your's, yours)

5. Louise practiced _____ speech for several days.   (her, hers)

6. Have you asked Mr. Hawkins about _____ taking the class pictures?   (him, his)

7. We couldn't decide whether to have the party at our house or _____. (their's, theirs)

8. _____ solution to the puzzle surprised everyone.   (My, Mine)

9. The dog returned the stick to _____ owner.   (it's, its)

10. We admired _____ cooking.   (them, their)

EXERCISE B: More Work with Pronouns in the Possessive Case. Write a possessive pronoun in the spaces provided to complete each of the sentences below.

EXAMPLE: ___*Our*___ team won the game.

1. Isn't this car _____?

2. Nearly every year _____ Ramblers are in the finals.

3. _____ doing the laundry so late at night woke up the family.

4. I want to know which of those notebooks is _____.

5. Danny begged Marcia to disclose _____ secret.

6. The storm left destruction in _____ wake.

7. The officers were charged with inappropriate tactics in _____ handling of the investigation.

8. Alice claimed that the book was _____.

9. Billy felt that _____ studying had paid off when he learned that he had passed the test.

10. The breeders were ecstatic when _____ horse won the race.

NAME _____ CLASS _____ DATE _____

11.2 Special Problems with Pronouns

Using Who and Whom Correctly

Who and *whoever* are nominative and are used for subjects and predicate nominatives. *Whom* and *whomever* are objective and are used for direct objects and objects of prepositions. For the possessive case, use *whose*, not *who's*.

THE CASES OF *WHO* AND *WHOEVER*	
Nominative	*Who* will bring the dessert? I will support *whoever* the candidate is.
Objective	*Whom* have you told? You may choose *whomever* you want to work with.
Possessive	*Whose* car is that?

Using Pronouns Correctly in Elliptical Clauses

In elliptical clauses beginning with *than* or *as,* use the form of the pronoun that you would use if the clause were fully stated.

Elliptical Clauses	Completed Clauses
Dan sings better than ___?___ . The boss paid Tim more than ___?___ . The coach helped him more than ___?___ .	Dan sings better than *I* [do]. The boss paid Tim more than [the boss paid] *me*. The coach helped him more than *I* [did]. The coach helped him more than [the coach helped] *me*.

EXERCISE A: Using *Who* and *Whom* Correctly. Write *who* or *whom* to complete each sentence.

EXAMPLE: Mr. Parker is the one ___*whom*___ I came to see.

1. _____ did the teacher appoint as monitor?
2. Lenny Jacobs is a coach _____ gets results.
3. The job is open to anyone _____ can speak German.
4. _____ is your favorite country singer?
5. A good baby-sitter must be someone _____ likes children.
6. _____ have you invited to the party?
7. _____ will attract more voters?
8. The police spoke to passers-by _____ had witnessed the accident.
9. That is the same woman _____ I saw at the rally.
10. Those are the actors _____ the director will audition.

EXERCISE B: Using Pronouns in Elliptical Clauses. Complete each sentence with an appropriate pronoun.

EXAMPLE: Tom is as tall as ___*I*___ .

1. Paul plays the piano better than _____.
2. The game pleased Sue as much as _____.
3. The judges chose Phil rather than _____.
4. I do not speak Spanish as well as _____.
5. That comment offended Jenny as much as _____.

12.1 Subject and Verb Agreement

Number: Singular and Plural

Number refers to the two forms of a word: singular and plural. Singular words indicate one; plural words indicate more than one.

NUMBER OF WORDS			
Part of Speech	Singular	Plural	Singular or Plural
Nouns	bakery woman	bakeries women	elk, trout, reindeer
Pronouns	I, he, she, it	we, they	you
Verbs	explores has, does am, is, was		(I, you, we, they) explore (I, you, we, they) have, do (you, we, they) are, were

Singular and Plural Subjects

A singular subject must have a singular verb. A plural subject must have a plural verb. A phrase or clause that interrupts a subject and its verb does not affect subject-verb agreement.

SUBJECT-VERB AGREEMENT	
Singular	Plural
John likes Chinese food. A vase of flowers is on the table. That reindeer has a red nose.	They prefer Italian cooking. The flowers in the vase are roses. Eight reindeer pull the sleigh.

EXERCISE A: Determining the Number of Words. Label each item below as *singular, plural,* or *both*.

EXAMPLE: have found ___both___

1. vegetables _____
2. were studying _____
3. deer _____
4. attorneys _____
5. closes _____

6. admire _____
7. children _____
8. spine _____
9. entertains _____
10. have lost _____

EXERCISE B: Making Subjects and Verbs Agree. Complete each sentence by writing the verb form given in the parentheses that agrees with the subject. Then label each sentence *S* if the subject is singular or *P* if it is plural.

EXAMPLE: Some members of that club ___do___ volunteer work. (do, does) ___P___

1. That musical by Rodgers and Hart _____ popular. (remain, remains) _____
2. Our neighbors at the end of the street _____ building a deck. (is, are) _____
3. The plants she likes best _____ tropical. (is, are) _____
4. The lawyer for the plaintiffs _____ more time. (need, needs) _____
5. That first edition of Frost's poems _____ valuable. (is, are) _____

12.1 Subject and Verb Agreement

Compound Subjects

A singular subject after *or* takes a singular verb. A plural subject after *or* takes a plural verb. Compound subjects joined by *and* take a plural verb unless they are thought of as one thing or modified by *every* or *each*.

	AGREEMENT WITH COMPOUND SUBJECTS
Joined by or or nor	Jason, Jen, or Pat *does* the dishes every night. Neither the Bombers nor the Raiders *are* likely to finish first. Either the owners or the realtor *has* the keys. Either the realtor or the owners *have* the keys.
Joined by and	Kim and Sally *are* coming for dinner. Dad and I *are* planning the menu. Chicken and dumplings *sounds* good. Every guest and family member *is* sure to enjoy it.

EXERCISE A: Compound Subjects Joined by *Or* or *Nor*. Write the verb form given in the parentheses that agrees with the subject in each sentence.

EXAMPLE: My parents or grandparents __*are*__ about to arrive. (is, are)

1. Neither the coach nor the players _____ much hope of winning. (holds, hold)

2. Mom or Dad _____ to my brother every night. (reads, read)

3. The leading actors or the director _____ the film on talk shows. (promotes, promote)

4. Lou, Dana, or Sam _____ ordered the pizza already. (has, have)

5. Lemonade, iced tea, or fruit juice _____ a refreshing drink. (is, are)

6. Aunt Ellen or my grandparents _____ for dinner every Sunday. (comes, come)

7. Neither Dan nor his father _____ golf very well. (plays, play)

8. Either a lesser-known singer or the star's back-up singers _____ up the audience. (warms, warm)

9. The principal or her assistants _____ detention. (supervises, supervise)

10. Donna or Marco _____ a good choice for student council. (is, are)

EXERCISE B: Compound Subjects Joined by *And*. Write the verb form given in the parentheses that agrees with the subject in each sentence.

EXAMPLE: Spaghetti and meatballs __*is*__ today's special. (is, are)

1. The director and stage manager _____ a meeting tomorrow. (has, have)

2. Every nook and cranny _____ thoroughly searched. (was, were)

3. Both the buyer and the seller _____ signed the contracts. (has, have)

4. The couch and draperies _____. (matches, match)

5. Bacon and eggs _____ Laura's favorite breakfast. (was, were)

12.1 Subject and Verb Agreement

Confusing Subjects

Always check certain kinds of subjects carefully to make sure they agree with their verbs.

AGREEMENT WITH CONFUSING SUBJECTS	
Subject After Verb	Atop each cookie *was* a fancy *candy*. Near the horizon *tower* the *masts* of the sailboats.
Subject Versus Predicate Nominative	*Cookies are* always a treat. A *treat* in our house *is* blueberry turnovers.
Collective Nouns	The *family camps* every summer. (as a group) The *family share* household chores. (as individuals)
Plural Form with Singular Meaning	*German measles is* also known as rubella. *Physics is* the science of matter and energy.
Amounts	Six *weeks is* the length of our health course. Two *yards* of fabric *sounds* like a lot.
Titles	*Two Gentlemen of Verona is* not often performed.
Indefinite Pronouns	*Either* of these scarves *matches*. (always singular) *Several* of these ties *are* stained. (always plural) *All* of the fabric *is* too bright. *All* of the chairs *need* slipcovers.

EXERCISE A: Deciding on the Number of Subjects. Assume that each item below is to be the subject of a sentence. Label each one *S* if it needs a singular verb or *P* if it needs a plural verb.

EXAMPLE: *Little Women*   _S_

1. Some of the tourists _____
2. Few of them _____
3. *The Three Musketeers* _____
4. Either of the students _____
5. Mumps _____

6. Each of the women _____
7. *Wuthering Heights* _____
8. One dollar _____
9. Both of the candidates _____
10. Some of the meat _____

EXERCISE B: Choosing Verbs to Agree with Difficult Subjects. Write the correct verb form in parentheses to complete each sentence.

EXAMPLE: Here _*are*_ the notes I borrowed. (is, are)

1. The World Series _____ played in October.   (is, are)
2. The group _____ disagreeing among themselves about the results.   (is, are)
3. Severe thunderstorms _____ a threat to life and property.   (is, are)
4. Half of the brownies _____ nuts in them.   (has, have)
5. The commission _____ its own chairperson.   (elects, elect)
6. The jury _____ polled individually.   (is, are)
7. The only difference between the dishes _____ the sauces.   (was, were)
8. There _____ always been a strong bond between us.   (has, have)
9. At the top of the bank _____ a mass of wildflowers.   (blooms, bloom)
10. *Romeo and Juliet* _____ not my favorite play.   (is, are)

12.2 Pronoun and Antecedent Agreement

Agreement Between Personal Pronouns and Antecedents

A personal pronoun must agree with its antecedent in person, number, and gender. Use a singular personal pronoun with two or more singular antecedents joined by *or* or *nor*. Use a plural personal pronoun with two or more antecedents joined by *and*. When dealing with pronoun-antecedent agreement, do not shift either person or gender. When gender is not specified, use the masculine or rewrite the sentence.

PRONOUN-ANTECEDENT AGREEMENT

My father has a CB radio in *his* truck.

This air mattress has a leak in *it*.

Francine got an A on *her* essay.

Beth or Ellen will have the party at *her* house.

Tim, Aaron, and Steve rode *their* bikes to the fair.

Each candidate stated *his* position clearly.

Both candidates expressed *their* positions clearly.

EXERCISE A: Choosing Personal Pronouns to Agree with Antecedents. Assume that each item below is an antecedent for a personal pronoun. After each, write *his, her, its,* or *their* to show which pronoun you would use to refer to it.

EXAMPLE: David or Goliath __*his*__

1. several parents _____
2. the new bike _____
3. either Jack or Bill _____
4. Pam, Ali, or Elise _____
5. only one woman _____

6. Erik and Marc _____
7. each actor _____
8. most experiments _____
9. the new report _____
10. the ballerina _____

EXERCISE B: Pronoun-Antecedent Agreement in Sentences. Write an appropriate personal pronoun to complete each sentence.

EXAMPLE: Pete and I enjoyed __*our*__ trip to Washington, D.C.

1. Although Ben had studied hard, _____ was still nervous about the test.
2. The pool is beautiful, but no one uses _____ .
3. Neither Dora nor Carol uses _____ calculator very often.
4. The candidate and her staff revised _____ travel plans.
5. Uncle Al takes _____ dog everywhere.
6. Pete hopes that _____ will get the part.
7. All students must show proof that _____ have been immunized.
8. Liz, may I borrow _____ history notes?
9. Mary has been practicing all week for _____ recital.
10. Maybe Chuck or Don will lend you _____ bike.

12.2 Pronoun and Antecedent Agreement

Agreement with Indefinite Pronouns

Use a singular personal pronoun when the antecedent is a singular indefinite pronoun. Use a plural personal pronoun when the antecedent is a plural indefinite pronoun. With an indefinite pronoun that can be either singular or plural, agreement depends on the antecedent of the indefinite pronoun.

AGREEMENT WITH INDEFINITE PRONOUNS
Each of my sisters has *her* own room.
Both of the players have *their* own distinctive styles.
Some of the bread has mold on *it*. (*bread* = singular antecedent)
Some of the students lost *their* note cards. (*students* = plural antecedent)

Agreement with Reflexive Pronouns

A reflexive pronoun must agree with an antecedent that is clearly stated.

REFLEXIVE PRONOUN AGREEMENT	
Incorrect	**Correct**
The new phone is for my brother and *myself*.	The new phone is for my brother and *me*.

EXERCISE A: Making Personal Pronouns Agree with Indefinite Pronouns. Write an appropriate personal pronoun to complete each sentence.

EXAMPLE: Neither of the doors has a lock on ___*it*___.

1. Most of this food has too much salt in _____.
2. Many of the players provide _____ own shin guards.
3. Few of the parents have given _____ permission.
4. Each of the windows has a candle in _____.
5. Anyone in the Boy Scout troop will lend you _____ handbook.
6. Several of my classmates have _____ own computers.
7. Little of the oceanfront property has houses on _____.
8. Somebody from the Women's Club will tell us about _____ hobby.
9. Do all of your books have your name in _____?
10. Some of the older records have scratches on _____.

EXERCISE B: Using Reflexive Pronouns Correctly. Underline the misused reflexive pronoun in each sentence. Write the correct pronoun on the line.

EXAMPLE: Both Carol and <u>yourself</u> have done a fine job.   ___*you*___

1. Jay lacks confidence in June and myself. _____
2. Grandma took my cousins and ourselves to the beach. _____
3. Please do not tell himself about this. _____
4. Jan bought a ticket for herself and yourself. _____
5. Donna and myself went out for dinner. _____

12.2 Pronoun and Antecedent Agreement

Four Special Problems in Pronoun Agreement

A personal pronoun should always have a clear, single, close, and logical antecedent, either stated or understood.

Problems	Corrections
They are predicting rain for tonight.	The forecasters are predicting rain for tonight.
Dad told Uncle Al that *he* had a flat tire.	Dad told Uncle Al that Dad had a flat tire. Dad told Uncle Al that Uncle Al had a flat tire.
Mom told Vera what *she* needed.	Mom told Vera what Mom needed. Mom told Vera what Vera needed.
In Paris *you* can see the Eiffel Tower.	Visitors to Paris can see the Eiffel Tower.

EXERCISE A: Solving Special Problems in Pronoun Agreement. Underline the word or words in parentheses that more clearly complete each sentence.

EXAMPLE: (They, The sportscasters) say the Cats don't stand a chance.

1. The rules specify that (you, entrants) must be 16 years of age.
2. Dad called Mr. Sims back as soon as (he, Dad) got home.
3. Please get the hamburgers and the napkins and put (them, the hamburgers) into the cooler.
4. The guards object if (you, visitors) touch the exhibits.
5. The scouts and their leaders decided that (they, the scouts) would sell candy bars.
6. On all flights (you, passengers) get first-class service.
7. The patient was relieved when (they, the doctors) told her the news.
8. Mr. Kelly told Bruce what (his, Bruce's) new job would involve.
9. Regular exercise is important to (your, everyone's) good health.
10. When will (they, the networks) begin the new season?

EXERCISE B: Correcting Special Problems in Pronoun Agreement. Rewrite each sentence below to correct any problems in pronoun agreement.

EXAMPLE: Tom told Ed that he should have known better.
      Tom told Ed that Ed should have known better.

1. What did they say when you called the hospital?

_____

2. That platter of food looks pretty with the parsley on it.

_____

3. In that ballet school, they expect you to practice four hours a day.

_____

4. Debby assured Maureen that her report would be excellent.

_____

5. Why do they tell you to keep your seatbelts loosely fastened?

_____

13.1 Degrees of Comparison

Recognizing Degrees of Comparison

Most adjectives and adverbs have three different forms to show degrees of comparison.

DEGREES OF COMPARISON			
	Positive	**Comparative**	**Superlative**
Adjectives	smooth luxurious many	smoother more luxurious more	smoothest most luxurious most
Adverbs	close rapidly far	closer more rapidly further	closest most rapidly furthest

Regular Forms

Use -er or more to form the comparative degree and -est or most to form the superlative degree of comparison of most one- and two-syllable modifiers. Use more and most to form the comparative and superlative degrees of all modifiers with three or more syllables.

REGULAR FORMS OF COMPARISON			
One- and two-syllable modifiers	strange crazy graceful	stranger crazier more graceful	strangest craziest most graceful
Three or more syllables	amazin g happily	more amazing more happily	most amazing most happily

EXERCISE A: Recognizing Degrees of Comparison. Identify the degree of comparison of the underlined word in each sentence by writing *pos.* (positive), *comp.* (comparative), or *sup.* (superlative).

EXAMPLE: Amy is <u>shorter</u> than her younger sister.   *comp.*

1. The baby's fever is <u>lower</u> this morning. _____

2. The weather has been perfectly <u>beautiful</u> all week. _____

3. This has been the <u>wettest</u> June on record. _____

4. The Jacksons' house is the <u>oldest</u> one on our street. _____

5. Kevin took the news <u>more calmly</u> than the rest of us. _____

6. The Smiths have the <u>most carefully</u> trimmed shrubs on the block. _____

7. The host greeted each guest <u>warmly</u>. _____

8. Pete just ate the <u>biggest</u> sandwich I had ever seen. _____

9. Louise felt <u>better</u> after she had talked things over. _____

10. The crowd gave an <u>enthusiastic</u> roar. _____

EXERCISE B: Comparing Adjectives and Adverbs. Write the missing forms of each modifier.

EXAMPLE: gloomy   *gloomier*   *gloomiest*

1. cautious   _____   _____

2. _____   _____   loudest

3. _____   more slowly   _____

4. soft   _____   _____

5. sadly   _____   _____

13.1 Degrees of Comparison

Irregular Forms

The irregular comparative and superlative forms of certain adjectives and adverbs must be memorized.

IRREGULAR MODIFIERS		
Positive	Comparative	Superlative
bad	worse	worst
badly	worse	worst
far (distance)	farther	farthest
far (extent)	further	furthest
good	better	best
ill	worse	worst
late	later	last *or* latest
little (amount)	less	least
many	more	most
much	more	most
well	better	best

EXERCISE A: Forming Irregular Comparative and Superlative Degrees. Write the appropriate form of the modifier in parentheses to complete each sentence.

EXAMPLE: The Bombers have a ___*better*___ chance of winning than the Stingers do. (good)

1. The dish he prepares _____ than any other is Beef Wellington. (well)

2. Perry swam _____ than anyone else on the team. (far)

3. Sadie's cold was even _____ the second day. (bad)

4. The _____ noise in the house keeps Chris awake. (little)

5. We caught the _____ train before the power went off. (late)

6. Mr. Pella said I should develop the second paragraph _____. (far)

7. That mosaic is the _____ thing I have ever made in art. (good)

8. Grandpa feels _____ today than yesterday. (ill)

9. Barnaby sang _____ of all when his throat was sore. (bad)

10. Some people need _____ sleep than others. (much)

EXERCISE B: Using Adjectives and Adverbs to Make Comparisons. Use each modifier in a sentence of your own that shows a clear comparison. Use three comparative forms and two superlatives.

EXAMPLE: (many) *Len has more clothes than anyone else I know.*

1. (bad) _____

2. (badly) _____

3. (good) _____

4. (little) _____

5. (well) _____

13.2 Clear Comparisons

Using Comparative and Superlative Degrees

Use the comparative degree to compare two people, places, things, or ideas. Use the superlative degree to compare three or more people, places, things, or ideas.

Comparative (comparing two)	Superlative (comparing three or more)
If you had called *earlier*, I could have talked. You will feel *better* after a nap. Jan is *more graceful* than her sister.	Jim arrived *earliest* of all the guests. I feel *best* after exercising. Jan is the *most graceful* dancer in the corps.

EXERCISE A: Using the Comparative and Superlative Degrees Correctly. Underline the correct form in each sentence.

EXAMPLE: Dad cooks (<u>better</u>, best) than Mom does.

1. All the rooms need painting, but the living room is the (less, least) dingy.
2. That white frame chapel is the (older, oldest) building in town.
3. Coastal regions usually have (more, most) moderate temperatures than the interior sections.
4. I wish I had proofread my essay (more carefully, most carefully).
5. Jenny has the (longer, longest) hair of anyone I know.
6. Timmy is a (more, most) active youngster than his brother.
7. The engine runs (more, most) smoothly since it was overhauled.
8. Latin IV has the (fewer, fewest) students of any class.
9. The SST is the (faster, fastest) passenger carrier.
10. Of the three candidates, Barker is the (more, most) likely to win.

EXERCISE B: Using the Comparative and Superlative Degrees in Sentences. Use each of the following modifiers in two sentences, first in the comparative degree and then in the superlative degree.

EXAMPLE: (pretty) *Cara's photographs are prettier than mine.*
 Daisy's photographs are the prettiest I have ever seen.

1. (successful) _____

 _____

2. (hard) _____

 _____

3. (young) _____

 _____

4. (tame) _____

 _____

5. (dangerous) _____

 _____

13.2 Clear Comparisons

Logical Comparisons

Make sure that your sentences compare only items of a similar kind.

Unbalanced Comparisons	Correct
This car rides smoother than *Dad*. A *parrot's plumage* is more colorful than *a parakeet*.	*This car* runs smoother than *Dad's*. A *parrot's plumage* is more colorful than *a parakeet's*.

When comparing one of a group with the rest of the group, use the word *other* or the word *else*.

Illogical	Correct
Gooden has a *higher* strike-out record *than any pitcher*. My brother always eats *more than anyone in our family*.	Gooden has a *higher* strike-out record *than any other pitcher*. My brother always eats *more than anyone else in our family*.

EXERCISE A: Making Balanced Comparisons. Rewrite each sentence, correcting the comparison.

EXAMPLE: My mosaic was larger than Jason.
  My mosaic was larger than Jason's.

1. Aunt Lena's spaghetti sauce is spicier than Mom.

   _____

2. Laura's corn has grown faster than Phil.

   _____

3. Ken's class picture was better than Mike.

   _____

4. Marc's clothes were even muddier than Steve.

   _____

5. Julie's job is more demanding than Hal.

   _____

EXERCISE B: Using *Other* and *Else* in Comparisons. Rewrite each sentence, correcting the comparison.

EXAMPLE: Audrey studies harder than anyone in the class.
  Audrey studies harder than anyone else in the class.

1. Often my homework takes me longer than anyone in my class.

   _____

2. That restaurant is more expensive than any place in town.

   _____

3. My friend Marcia writes better than anyone I know.

   _____

4. The intersection at Elm and Main is more dangerous than any in town.

   _____

5. Is there anyone who works as hard as Eric?

   _____

14.1 Negative Sentences

Recognizing Double Negatives

Do not write sentences with double negatives.

Double Negatives	Correct Negative Sentences
I *haven't* seen *no one*.	I *haven't* seen anyone. I have seen *no one*.
I *haven't* done *nothing* wrong.	I *haven't* done anything wrong. I have done *nothing* wrong.
We *don't* have *no* school today.	We *don't* have school today. We have *no* school today.

Forming Negative Sentences Correctly

Use only one negative word in a single clause. Do not use *but* in its negative sense with another negative. Do not use *barely, hardly,* or *scarcely* with another negative.

More Double Negatives	Correct Negative Sentences
Didn't Ann say she *couldn't* find *nobody*?	Didn't Ann say she *couldn't* find anybody? Didn't Ann say she could find *nobody*?
I *haven't but* a dollar.	I have *but* a dollar. I *haven't* more than a dollar.
We *didn't* have *hardly* any food left.	We had *hardly* any food left. We *didn't* have any food left.

EXERCISE A: Avoiding Problems with Negatives. Underline the word(s) in parentheses that make each sentence negative without creating a double negative.

EXAMPLE: I couldn't find my keys (<u>anywhere</u>, nowhere).

1. You shouldn't have told (anybody, nobody) where we were going.
2. We (could, couldn't) hardly make our way through the brush.
3. Are you sure you (don't have, have) but one day free this week?
4. There wasn't (a, no) cloud in the sky.
5. Jo didn't have (any, no) trouble choosing a topic.
6. The article didn't include (any, no) biographical information.
7. I don't have room for (but, more than) one elective in my schedule.
8. Kelly can't (ever, never) finish anything on time.
9. There (was, wasn't) scarcely enough breeze to ruffle a leaf.
10. I have hardly (ever, never) been more moved by a play.

EXERCISE B: Using Negatives Correctly. Write a sentence of your own, correctly using each negative word given.

EXAMPLE: (hardly)   _Jimmy hardly ever eats between meals._

1. (nothing) _____
2. (but) _____
3. (wouldn't) _____
4. (barely) _____
5. (never) _____

14.2 Sixty Common Usage Problems

Solving Usage Problems

Study the items in the usage glossary in your textbook, paying particular attention to similar spellings, words that should never be used, pairs that are often misused, and problems with verb forms.

TYPES OF PROBLEMS		
Similar Spellings	all ready and already	farther and further
Wrong Words	alot	enthused
Misused Pairs	anxious and eager	teach and learn
Verb Forms	busted for burst	of for have

EXERCISE A: Avoiding Common Usage Problems. Underline the word in parentheses that correctly completes each sentence.

EXAMPLE: I would (advice, <u>advise</u>) you to be careful what you say to him.

1. The real painting looks quite different (from, than) the reproductions.
2. Because I had (laid, lay, lain) in the sun too long, my skin felt tight.
3. I would (have, of) gotten here sooner if the car hadn't broken down.
4. The new tax bill would (affect, effect) all income levels.
5. The candidate mingled (among, between) the guests at the benefit.
6. Nick watches television endlessly, (irregardless, regardless) of what is on.
7. Last weekend our team (beat, won) the Raiders again.
8. Proper food, rest, and exercise help build (healthful, healthy) bodies.
9. I heard (that, where) the Keenans are moving to Detroit.
10. Did your uncle (learn, teach) you that magic trick?

EXERCISE B: Avoiding Other Usage Problems. Underline the word(s) in parentheses that correctly complete each sentence.

EXAMPLE: Marcia's ideas (<u>about</u>, as to) decorations sounded exciting.

1. We were all (anxious, eager) to begin our vacation.
2. The press has given (all together, altogether) too much attention to the candidate's family.
3. By the time we arrived, there was (nowhere, nowheres) to sit.
4. The van driver (sat, set) the old woman's packages on her porch.
5. (Because, Being that) we overslept, Mom drove us to school.
6. Harry was surprised that his parents (left, let) him go on the trip.
7. Students (that, which) have permission slips may go on the trip.
8. I was surprised that little Teddy could walk such a long (way, ways).
9. Damian studies harder (than, then) many of his classmates.
10. Hilda's grandparents (emigrated, immigrated) from Germany.

15.1 Rules for Capitalization

Rules for Capitalization

Capitalize the first word in a sentence, including complete sentences in quotations and following a colon. Capitalize the first word in interjections and incomplete questions, as well as the words *I* and *O*. Capitalize the first word in each line of most poetry.

CAPITALS FOR FIRST WORDS	
Complete Sentences	When can we expect delivery? What a fright you gave me!
Quoted Sentence	The chief shouted, "Sound the alarm."
Sentence After Colon	One thing seems clear: We must act at once.
Interjection	Darn! He left his wallet in his locker.
Incomplete Question	What time?
I and *O*	Today, O spring, I claim you for myself.
Lines of Poetry	Not marble, nor the gilded monuments Of princes, shall outlive this powerful rhyme.

EXERCISE A: Using Capitals for First Words. Underline the word or words that should be capitalized in each sentence.

EXAMPLE: <u>after</u> dinner <u>i</u> asked, "<u>what's</u> for dessert?"

1. only one solution is possible: we must cut our expenses.
2. what a beautiful sunset we had last night!
3. the tourist asked, "does the Number 4 bus stop here?"
4. that restaurant deserves its reputation, i think.
5. ouch! that rose bush is loaded with thorns.
6. of course i'll meet you after school. but where?
7. a volunteer listed the victims' needs: food, clothing, and blankets are the greatest needs at present.
8. one student suggested, "couldn't we raise money with a bake sale?"
9. halfway through the movie i began wondering, "when will this end?"
10. several of my classmates are going to computer camp this summer.

EXERCISE B: Using Capitalized Words. Fill in each blank with an appropriate capitalized word.

EXAMPLE: Tony suggested, "__*Certainly*__ the town needs a recycling center."

1. _____ did you last see my keys?
2. The teacher said, "_____ your work carefully."
3. The effects of the storm were devastating: _____ trees and other debris were everywhere.
4. _____ can tell me how to get there?
5. James exclaimed, "_____! What a lucky break that was!"
6. _____ parents are very supportive.
7. The situation is this: _____ must find a new source of income.
8. _____ is a good source of calcium.
9. Jessica wondered, "_____ could have left that message?"
10. _____ boy blue, come blow your horn.

   _____ sheep's in the meadow; the cow's in the corn.

15.1 Rules for Capitalization

Capitals for Proper Nouns

Capitalize proper nouns, including each important word in a proper noun of more than one word.

PROPER NOUNS	
Name of People: James A. McCoy	*Geographical Names:* Cedar Street
Names of Animals: Lassie	*Specific Places:* the Chrysler Building
Specific Events: the War of 1812	*Specific Groups:* League of Nations
Religious Terms: Bible	*Awards:* the Cy Young Award
Specific Vehicles: the *Concorde*	*Brand Names:* Atari

Capitals for Proper Adjectives

Capitalize most proper adjectives.

PROPER ADJECTIVES	
With Capitals	**Without Capitals**
Proper Adjectives: Chinese food	*Common Terms:* venetian blinds
Brand Names: Yamaha motorcycle	*Most Prefixes:* pro-British sentiment
Combinations: Judeo-Christian tradition	*Parts of Compounds:* French-speaking province

EXERCISE A: Recognizing Proper Nouns and Proper Adjectives. Underline the proper nouns and proper adjectives in each sentence. Rewrite each one correctly on the line at the right.

EXAMPLE: We visited the <u>tower of london</u> last <u>july</u>. _Tower of London   July_

1. In texas we saw the rio grande and the alamo. _____

2. That hemingway novel is set during the spanish civil war. _____

3. Will the talks reduce soviet-american tensions? _____

4. Did alex order french fries or a baked potato? _____

5. My neighbor mrs. henderson drives a green chevrolet. _____

6. The league of women voters sponsored the debate. _____

7. Those japanese tourists seem very pro-american. _____

8. The koran is the holy book of islam. _____

9. The baseball hall of fame is in cooperstown, new york. _____

10. We met many english-speaking russians on our trip. _____

EXERCISE B: Using Proper Nouns and Proper Adjectives. Fill in each blank with a proper noun or proper adjective.

EXAMPLE: The __Alps__ and the __Urals__ are mountain ranges in __Europe__ .

1. My parents are considering buying a (n) _____ computer.

2. The tour will include stops in _____ and
   _____ .

3. Several speakers expressed pro- _____ views.

4. I have just finished reading a book by _____ .

5. Our state capital is _____ .

6. The biggest event in baseball is the _____ .

7. Will you ask _____ and _____
   to join us?

8. We went skiing in the _____ .

9. The coldest continent is _____ .

15.1 Rules for Capitalization

Capitals for Titles

Capitalize titles of people and titles of works.

People	Works
Social: Lord and Lady Grantford *Business:* Superintendent Meyers *Military:* Captain McGrath *Government:* Mayor Jane Sims *Religious:* Rabbi Feldman *Compound:* Commander in Chief *Abbreviations:* Dr., Mrs., Jr., Ph.D.	*Book:* Peter Rabbit *Periodical:* Reader's Digest *Poem:* "The Raven" *Story:* "A Day's Wait" *Painting:* Christina's World *Music:* The Nutcracker Suite *Courses:* English Composition II

Capitals in Letters

Capitalize the first word and all nouns in letter salutations and the first word in letter closings.

	Salutations	Closings
	Dear Aunt Eleanor, Dear Senator Williams: My dear Friend,	Your loving niece, Sincerely yours, Yours truly,

EXERCISE A: Using Capitals in Titles. Underline the words that should be capitalized in each sentence.

EXAMPLE: *The prime of miss jean brodie* is set in a girls' boarding school.

1. Has major adams approved the plan?
2. Have you ever read "the ransom of red chief"?
3. Some of the world's most precious jewels belong to the queen of england.
4. We heard professor harold jenkins lecture on politics last night.
5. That is a reproduction of *the last supper*.
6. Leon has misplaced his script for *arsenic and old lace*.
7. The new pastor is father riley.
8. Either mrs. pauling or dr. o'rourke will make the presentation.
9. Have you seen a copy of *undersea world,* the new scuba diving magazine?
10. The first selection will be handel's *water music*.

EXERCISE B: Using Capitals for Salutations and Closings. Rewrite each of the following letter parts, adding the missing capitals.

EXAMPLE: dear uncle albert, ___*Dear Uncle Albert,*___

1. dear dr. morgan, _____
2. with deep affection, _____
3. gratefully, _____
4. my dear cousin, _____
5. very truly yours, _____
6. dear professor atkins: _____
7. yours sincerely, _____
8. dear sir or madam: _____
9. my dear marian, _____
10. with all good wishes, _____

15.2 Rules for Abbreviation

Names and Titles of People

Abbreviated titles before and after proper names begin with a capital letter and end with a period. Social titles and the title *Dr.* may be used with just a last name in formal writing. Other abbreviations should be used only with a full name.

Social Titles	Other Titles	Titles After Names
Mrs. Scott	Dr. Gordon	Harding Lewis, Jr.
Messrs. Reading and Thomson	Gen. Elson V. Terry	Renata Antonio, Ph.D.

Geographical Terms

Abbreviations for geographical terms before or after a proper noun begin with a capital letter and end with a period. Traditional abbreviations for states begin and end with a capital and end with a period. The Postal Service abbreviations are all capitals with no periods. Abbreviations for geographical terms are generally not used in formal writing.

GEOGRAPHICAL TERMS			
Building	Bldg.	Province	Prov.
Arizona	Ariz. (traditional)	AZ	(Postal Service)
Illinois	Ill. (traditional)	IL	(Postal Service)
Vermont	Vt. (traditional)	VT	(Postal Service)

EXERCISE A: Using Abbreviations for Titles of People and Geographical Terms. On the line at the right, write the correct abbreviation for the word or words in parentheses. If the abbreviation can be used in formal writing, put a (√) next to it.

EXAMPLE: (Mister) Raymond A. Harding is my uncle.   ___Mr.√___

1. (Reverend) Feltcher has been at the same church for twenty years.   _____

2. My mother's office is next to Anna Sims, (Doctor of Medicine).   _____

3. Lenny's house is on Woodcut (Road).   _____

4. (Lieutenant) Bardo was sent to Japan.   _____

5. We visited (Mount) McKinley last July.   _____

6. Wendy lives on Madison (Avenue).   _____

7. (Senator) Dennis Parks will be our guest speaker.   _____

8. I always enjoy (Professor) Bailey's lectures.   _____

9. They have renamed the road Ella Grasso (Boulevard).   _____

10. (Doctor) Craig is unable to come to the phone.   _____

EXERCISE B: More Work with Abbreviations. Next to each item, write the correct abbreviation.

EXAMPLE: Representative ___Rep.___

1. Maryland (Postal Service) _____
2. Doctor of Philosophy _____
3. California (traditional) _____
4. Drive _____
5. Nebraska (traditional) _____
6. Bachelor of Arts _____
7. Rhode Island (Postal Service) _____
8. Ambassador _____
9. Registered Nurse _____
10. Maine (traditional) _____

15.2 Rules for Abbreviation

Time, Measurements, and Numbers

Abbreviations for clocked time begin with a small letter, but those for days of the week and months begin with a capital. All three end with a period. Abbreviations of time before and after noon are formed with capital letters or small letters followed by periods. Abbreviations for historical dates before and after the birth of Christ require capital letters followed by periods.

TIME ABBREVIATIONS			
sec.	second(s)	Mon.	Monday
Jan.	January	A.M. or a.m.	before noon
Feb.	February	B.C.	Before Christ

Traditional measurements use small letters and periods to form abbreviations; those for metric measurements generally use small letters and no periods. In formal writing, spell out numbers of amounts of less than one hundred and any other numbers that can be written in one or two words.

MEASUREMENTS					
Traditional Measurements				**Metric Measurements**	
in. inch(es)		yd. yard(s)		cm centimeter(s)	kg kilogram(s)
tsp. teaspoon(s)		oz. ounce(s)		g gram(s)	L liter(s)

EXERCISE A: Recognizing the Meanings of Abbreviations. Write out the word or words that each abbreviation stands for.

EXAMPLE: Jan. _____January_____

1. B.C. _____
2. mi. _____
3. mm _____
4. lb. _____
5. pt. _____

6. tsp. _____
7. hr. _____
8. kL. _____
9. Feb. _____
10. Wed. _____

EXERCISE B: More Work with Abbreviations. Write the appropriate abbreviation for each of the words below.

EXAMPLE: teaspoon _____tsp._____

1. inches _____
2. September _____
3. Before Christ _____
4. liter _____
5. June _____
6. after noon _____
7. meters _____
8. second _____
9. November _____
10. Celsius _____

11. August _____
12. pounds _____
13. Fahrenheit _____
14. miles _____
15. Sunday _____
16. minutes _____
17. quart _____
18. October _____
19. milliliters _____
20. pint _____

15.2 Rules for Abbreviation

Latin Expressions

Use small letters and periods for most Latin abbreviations.

LATIN EXPRESSIONS			
c., ca., circ.	about (used to show approximate dates)	i.e.	that is
e.g.	for example	etc.	and so forth

Other Abbreviations

An abbreviated word in a business name begins with a capital letter and ends with a period. Use all capitals and no periods to abbreviate names that are pronounced letter by letter as well as for acronyms that form names.

OTHER ABBREVIATIONS			
Co.	Company	Ltd.	Limited
FCC	Federal Communications Commission	NATO	North Atlantic Treaty Organization

EXERCISE A: Identifying the Meanings of Abbreviations. Write out the word or words that each abbreviation stands for.

EXAMPLE: IRS ___*Internal Revenue Service*___

1. Bros. _____
2. TWA _____
3. Corp. _____
4. NFL _____
5. Inc. _____

6. e.g. _____
7. VP _____
8. et al. _____
9. Ltd. _____
10. i.e. _____

EXERCISE B: Using Abbreviations. Next to each item, write the correct abbreviation.

EXAMPLE: Company ___Co.___

1. National Basketball Association _____
2. Manufacturing _____
3. and so forth _____
4. North Atlantic Treaty Organization _____
5. and the following (page or line) _____
6. Columbia Broadcasting System _____
7. Young Men's Christian Association _____
8. National Aeronautics and Space Administration _____
9. for example _____
10. and _____

16.1 End Marks

Basic Uses of End Marks

Use a period (.) to end a declarative sentence, a mild imperative, and an indirect question. Use a question mark (?) to end a direct question, an incomplete question, or a statement intended as a question. Use an exclamation mark (!) to end an exclamatory sentence, a forceful imperative sentence, or an interjection expressing strong emotion.

Periods	Question Marks	Exclamation Marks
The sky is clear today.	Is it sunny outside?	How clear the sky is!
Just put your coat here.	What time?	Go for help!
She asked if I was ready.	We really won?	Ouch! That hurt!

Other Uses of End Marks

Use a period to end most abbreviations and after numbers and letters in outlines. Use a question mark in parentheses (?) after a fact or statistic to show its uncertainty.

Periods	Question Marks
Mr. L. A. Ransom, Ph.D.	The group raised $25.80(?).
I. Causes of revolt	On January 21 (?) the group
A. Pay inequities	will have its first meeting.

EXERCISE A: Using End Marks for Sentences and Phrases. Write the proper end mark at the end of each item.

EXAMPLE: You're kidding. She really said that ___?___

1. What a magnificent performance that was _____

2. Are you going to the game on Saturday _____

3. I wonder how big the crowd will be _____

4. Pete won first prize. Yeah _____

5. Don't ever do that again _____

6. Louis ordered another pizza _____

7. How amazing that such a young child can read so well _____

8. The waiter asked if we wanted dessert _____

9. Don't forget to take your umbrella _____

10. What time is the train due _____

EXERCISE B: Using End Marks in Your Own Sentences. Follow the directions to write your own sentences.

EXAMPLE: Write a sentence that contains an interjection.
        Gee! I made a dumb mistake.

1. Write a sentence that suggests uncertainty about a date.

_____

2. Write a sentence that includes an abbreviated title.

_____

3. Write a statement intended as a question.

_____

4. Write a forceful imperative sentence.

_____

16.2 Commas

Commas with Compound Sentences

Use a comma before the conjunction to separate two independent clauses in a compound sentence.

COMPOUND SENTENCES
We worked most of the day, but we didn't finish painting the room. Not only were we late for the party, but most of the food was gone also.

Commas with Series and Adjectives

Use commas to separate three or more words, phrases, or clauses in a series. Use commas to separate adjectives of equal rank but not to separate adjectives that must stay in a specific order.

With Commas	Without Commas
Mom bought chocolate, milk, and cookies for the party.	Mom bought milk and cookies for the party.
Eager, devoted fans waited outside the star's dressing room.	Many eager fans waited outside the star's dressing room.

EXERCISE A: Using Commas Correctly. Add commas where they are needed. One sentence needs no commas.

EXAMPLE: My chores include cleaning my room, dusting the living room, and taking out the trash.

 1. The actor delivered the soliloquy in a clear strong voice.
 2. My sister goes to college in Ohio and my brother goes to college in Maine.
 3. Parsley sprigs lemon slices and tomato wedges formed an attractive border on the platter.
 4. The hot tired campers headed straight for the lake.
 5. Janice may bake a cake or we can order one at Farella's.
 6. Have you seen the Jacksons' three new puppies?
 7. Our trip was far from perfect but at least we got home safely.
 8. Elmer saw a large lumpy figure moving through the shadows.
 9. Jeremy had planned a special meal but it was ruined.
10. Will you fly take the train or drive to California?

EXERCISE B: Understanding Rules for Commas. Describe the comma rule for each sentence in Exercise A above by writing *compound sentence, series, equal adjectives,* or *adjectives in order.*

EXAMPLE: _series_

 1. _____

 2. _____

 3. _____

 4. _____

 5. _____

 6. _____

 7. _____

 8. _____

 9. _____

10. _____

16.2 Commas

Commas After Introductory Material

Use a comma after an introductory word, phrase, or clause.

INTRODUCTORY MATERIAL
Introductory Word: Yes, that is the book I ordered.
Introductory Phrase: Without a word to anyone, Susan left the house.
Introductory Clause: As the ship sailed away, we waved at Jim.

Commas with Parenthetical and Nonessential Expressions

Use commas to set off parenthetical and nonessential expressions.

PARENTHETICAL EXPRESSIONS
Names of People Being Addressed: Did you know, Tom, that I am a twin?
Certain Adverbs: We hoped, however, that the weather would improve.
Common Expressions: The outcome, in my opinion, looks bleak.
Contrasting Expressions: Those scrolls are from China, not Korea.

Essential Expressions	Nonessential Expressions
My friend the football player is trying for a scholarship.	Jack, a football player, is trying for a scholarship.
The woman now approaching the microphone will introduce the speaker.	Alice, now approaching the microphone, will introduce the speaker.

EXERCISE A: Recognizing Introductory Material. Write the introductory word, phrase, or clause in each sentence, and add the needed comma.

EXAMPLE: Actually I would rather stay home.   *Actually,*

1. Yes the crocuses have begun to bloom. _____

2. To win the game we need a miracle. _____

3. Shrugging her shoulders Melody walked away. _____

4. Before we knew it the movie ended. _____

5. Exhausted we looked for a shady spot to rest. _____

6. Although he works hard math is difficult for Bob. _____

7. As soon as we got your call we changed our plans. _____

8. Alice have you seen my keys anywhere? _____

9. To get to work Mom takes a bus and a train. _____

10. Frankly I have my doubts about the proposal. _____

EXERCISE B: Using Commas with Parenthetical and Nonessential Expressions. Add commas where they are needed. One sentence needs no commas.

EXAMPLE: My mother, a doctor, hopes that I will follow in her footsteps.

1. It was Bill not Bob whom I met at the concert.

2. The novel *All the King's Men* is set in Louisiana.

3. We agreed of course that the party should be a surprise.

4. Mr. Palmeri our next-door neighbor grows beautiful roses.

5. T. S. Eliot who was born in St. Louis adopted England as his home.

16.2 Commas

Other Uses of the Comma

When a date, a geographical name, or an address is made up of two or more parts, use a comma after each item except in the case of a month followed by a day. Use commas to set off a title following a name. Also use commas in the other situations shown in the chart below.

Date	On April 18, 1775, Paul Revere made his famous ride.
Geographical Name	Atlanta, Georgia, was almost totally destroyed by fire during the Civil War.
Address	We are moving to 1678 Main Street, Akron, Ohio.
Name with Title	Alice Evans, Ph.D., will speak on Monday.
Salutation and Closing	Dear Aunt Eleanor, Your loving niece,
Numbers	37,500 1,675,758
Elliptical Sentence	Jake excels at baseball; Mike, at basketball.
Direct Quotation	"Soon," mused Paul, "this day will be over."
To Prevent Confusion	Together with Julie, Erin is going to the ballet.

EXERCISE A: Adding Commas to Sentences. Insert commas where they are needed.

EXAMPLE: Lorraine Hall R.N. will teach the CPR course.
            Lorraine Hall, R.N., will teach the CPR course.

1. That family has moved to 721 Barker Street Jefferson Missouri.
2. John ordered swordfish; Paul fried clams.
3. The station's goal is 1235 new subscribers.
4. Jed asked "Is February 13 a good day for the party?"
5. Sarah Marsh L.P.N. prefers hospital work to private duty in homes.
6. Without Ellen Ann was lonely.
7. On June 12 1985 my grandfather will celebrate his sixtieth birthday.
8. The new hotel has 1354 rooms.
9. "Whenever you are ready" Pat called "we can leave."
10. After dinner entertainment will be offered.

EXERCISE B: Punctuating a Letter. Add commas wherever necessary in the following letter.

> 629 West 4th Street
> Montpelier Vermont 05602
> December 4 1984

Dear Paulette

Your letter was waiting for me when we arrived home on Friday November 30 after a short trip. We had gone to Boston Massachusetts to spend Thanksgiving with my grandparents.

It was odd that you should have asked for Margie's address. I just got a letter from her, too—the first one since her family moved on August 1 1983. Her address is Margaret Bayard 289 South Caxton Place Gettysburg Pennsylvania.

Your plan for a reunion this summer sounds wonderful! I wonder if Beth will be able to come 1700 miles for it though. But as you always used to say "Let's go for it!" Keep me posted on the plans.

> Your old friend
> Sonya

16.3 Semicolons and Colons

Uses of the Semicolon

Use a semicolon to join independent clauses not already joined by a coordinating conjunction or those separated by a conjunctive adverb or transitional expression. Use semicolons to avoid confusion when independent clauses already contain commas or between items in a series that contains commas.

With Independent Clauses	The chief sounded the alarm; the firefighters raced to their stations.
With a Conjunctive Adverb	Helene has a 4.0 average; consequently, she has a good chance for a scholarship.
With a Transitional Expression	In the first place, Stan loves all sports; in addition, he has excellent coordination.
With Items That Already Have Commas	The judges will include Ms. Haley, the drama coach; Mr. Dakin, the choral director; and Mr. Odem, the local drama critic.

EXERCISE A: Using Semicolons Correctly. In each sentence a comma is used instead of a semicolon. Circle the comma to show that a semicolon is needed.

EXAMPLE: Jenny has neglected her studies lately⊙ consequently, her grades are falling.

1. Since childhood Amy has loved animals, therefore, her career as a veterinarian is hardly surprising.
2. Cucumbers, carrots, tomatoes, and onions are common in salads, but have you ever tried adding broccoli, eggplant, or corn?
3. When Anna is home from college, all the bedrooms are full, but we can always put up a guest in the playroom, a room that is seldom used.
4. Just put the packages on the porch, we'll have to wait here until someone gets home with the key.
5. Penny had just come off a twelve-hour shift, she was exhausted.
6. We are to supply paper goods, beverages, and snacks, but Tom will provide the main dish, the vegetables, and the salad.
7. The house needs to be painted, in addition, it needs a new roof.
8. This is an ideal time to start out, the roads are not yet crowded.
9. Jason, whom I have known all my life, was a very serious youngster, but he has, surprisingly enough, become the life of every party.
10. Grandma has lived in that old house all her life, no wonder she doesn't want to move.

EXERCISE B: Understanding Uses of the Semicolon. Give the reason why each of the semicolons in Exercise A above is needed by writing the appropriate label from the chart.

EXAMPLE: _conjunctive adverb_

1. _____   6. _____
2. _____   7. _____
3. _____   8. _____
4. _____   9. _____
5. _____   10. _____

16.3 Semicolons and Colons

Uses of the Colon

Use a colon to introduce a list of items after an independent clause; a quotation that is formal, lengthy, or lacking a "he said/she said" expression; a sentence that summarizes or explains the sentence before it; or a formal appositive that follows an independent clause.

INTRODUCTORY COLONS	
List	The arrangement consisted entirely of spring flowers: iris, daffodils, tulips, and hyacinths.
Quotation	Ellen waved goodbye: "Have a good trip."
Summary Sentence	The paper reported the election results: All three present school board members were unseated.
Formal Appositive	The class play will be an American classic: *Our Town*.

In addition, use a colon in the following special situations.

OTHER USES OF THE COLON	
Numerals Giving Time	8:17 A.M. 11:57 P.M.
Periodical References	*National Geographic* XI: 421 (volume: page)
Biblical References	I Corinthians 13: 4–13 (chapter: verse[s])
Subtitles	*Pierre: A Cautionary Tale*
Salutations in Business Letters	Dear Ms. Adamson: Gentlemen:
Labels Signaling Important Ideas	Caution: Keep this and all medications out of the reach of children.

EXERCISE A: Using Colons Correctly. Add colons where they are needed in the following sentences.

EXAMPLE: The recipe calls for three basic spices garlic, parsley, and thyme.
            The recipe calls for three basic spices: garlic, parsley, and thyme.

1. Jeremy unfolded the note "Meet me in the gym after school."
2. The express, which was due at 8 14, did not arrive until 9 00 P.M.
3. Two actors have refused Academy Awards George C. Scott and Marlon Brando.
4. The three magazines with the largest paid subscriptions last year were these *TV Guide, Reader's Digest,* and *National Geographic Magazine.*
5. Warning This cabinet contains dangerous electrical equipment.

EXERCISE B: More Work with Colons. Follow the directions in Exercise A.

1. The text of the sermon was Matthew 10 8.
2. I am reporting on a biography entitled *Gandhi Fighter Without a Sword*.
3. Caution Read this manual completely before using your power sled.
4. Flight 401 leaves LaGuardia Airport at 8 40 A.M. each weekday.
5. The president banged the gavel "Let the meeting come to order."

16.4 Quotation Marks with Direct Quotations

Direct Quotations

A direct quotation represents a person's exact speech or thoughts and is enclosed in quotation marks (" "). An indirect quotation reports only the general meaning of what a person said or thought and does not require quotation marks. In writing direct quotations, use a comma or colon after an introductory expression and a comma, question mark, or exclamation mark after a quotation followed by a concluding expression. Also use commas to surround interrupting expressions in a direct quotation. Use a comma, question mark, or exclamation mark after a quoted sentence before an interrupting expression and a period after the expression.

Direct Quotations	Indirect Quotations
"Do you think that it will rain?" asked Harry.	Harry wondered whether or not it would rain.
Harry asked, "Do you think that it will rain?"	Harry asked me if I thought it would rain.
"I certainly hope," Cheryl said, "that we will win the game."	Cheryl hoped that we would win the game.
"Slow down!" Max exclaimed. "There's an accident ahead."	Max told the driver to slow down because there was an accident ahead.

EXERCISE A: Distinguishing Between Direct and Indirect Quotations. Label each sentence below *D* (for direct quotation) or *I* (for indirect quotation).

EXAMPLE: All I know, Sharon said, is that I did my best.   ___D___

1. The tourist asked for directions to the World Trade Center. _____

2. Marcia began her letter: Dear Santa, Please bring me a new sled. _____

3. Have you chosen your topic for the report? Darryl inquired. _____

4. Bruce told me not to tell anyone about the party. _____

5. We could go roller skating, Dana suggested, or would you rather see a movie? _____

6. The garden really needs weeding, Mom observed. _____

7. I told the waiter to bring me another fork. _____

8. Amanda suggested that we could organize a scrap paper drive. _____

9. Ouch! Lou cried. That pan is hot! _____

10. The librarian said that our entire card catalog will soon be on a computer. _____

EXERCISE B: Using Quotation Marks Correctly. In each sentence labeled *D* above, add quotation marks where they are needed. Rewrite below each sentence labeled *I* so that it contains a direct quotation. Use quotation marks where they are needed.

EXAMPLE: _"All I know," Sharon said, "is that I did my best."_

1. _____

2. _____

3. _____

4. _____

5. _____

16.4 Quotation Marks with Direct Quotations

Other Punctuation Marks with Quotation Marks

Always place a comma or a period inside the final quotation marks. Always place a semicolon or colon outside the final quotation marks. Use the meaning of the whole sentence to determine the placement of question marks and exclamation marks.

PLACING OTHER PUNCTUATION MARKS	
Commas and Periods	"I am sure," Beth said, "that you are right."
Colons and Semicolons	Jill remarked, "We have a problem"; she went on to give details.
Question Marks and Exclamation Marks	Nina asked, "Isn't she the one?" Didn't Nina say, "She is the one"?

Quotation Marks in Special Situations

Use single quotation marks for a quotation within a quotation. When writing dialogue, begin a new paragraph with each change of speaker. For quotations longer than a paragraph, put quotation marks at the beginning of each paragraph and at the end of the final paragraph.

SPECIAL USES OF QUOTATION MARKS	
Quotation Within a Quotation	Ann answered, "The soliloquy begins, 'To be or not to be,' and it is found in Act III of *Hamlet*."

Dialogue	"Pets are well known to offer benefits to humans. They provide companionship, loyalty, and affection without making difficult emotional demands.
	   "Pets are particularly beneficial," the psychologist continued, "at times of great loss."
	   "However," interrupted the allergist, "there are medical hazards from pets as well."

EXERCISE A: Punctuating Direct Quotations. In each sentence punctuation marks are missing. Add them correctly to the sentences.

EXAMPLE: Jed asked, Who wrote the line Hope springs eternal?
           Jed asked, *"Who wrote the line 'Hope springs eternal'?"*

1. Didn't the travel agent say, All tips are included in the package price?
2. Jeffrey remarked, She should be here any minute; then the doorbell rang.
3. I wonder, Phyllis mused, if we have taken the right action.
4. Who ordered the pizza? Kelly asked.
5. The patient winced, That felt like more than just the prick of a pin!
6. I remember, Grandma reminisced, the day when you were born.
7. Do you think, Mom asked, that we need more cookies?
8. Have you ever wondered, the teacher asked, who first said, Eureka?
9. Carmen announced loudly, I'm starved; just then the waiter arrived.
10. Perhaps, Phil suggested, we should postpone the party.

EXERCISE B: Paragraphing Dialogue. Write a short dialogue between you and a friend on a topic below or another of your choice. Have one of the speakers go on for more than a single paragraph.

an upcoming school function   a current movie   studying for an important test
a political issue in your town   a book you have recently read   finding a summer job

16.5 Underlining and Other Uses of Quotation Marks

Underlining

Underline the titles of books, plays, periodicals, newspapers, long poems, movies, radio and TV series, long musical compositions, albums, and works of art. In addition, underline the names of individual air, sea, space, and land craft; foreign words not yet accepted into English; numbers, symbols, letters, and words used to name themselves; and words that you want to stress.

Titles	Other Uses
Wuthering Heights (novel)	the Concorde (plane)
The Miracle Worker (play)	the Montrealer (train)
Return of the Jedi (movie)	I will keep you au courant.
Family Ties (TV series)	That t should be capitalized.
Madama Butterfly (opera)	Check the spelling of chief.
the Thinker (sculpture)	Please leave now!

Quotation Marks

Use quotation marks for the titles of short written works, parts of longer works, songs, and works that are part of a collection.

WORKS WITH QUOTATION MARKS	
"A Day's Wait" (short story)	"Out of My Dreams" (song)
"Ile" (one-act play)	"Floods of Gold" (chapter)
"Mending Wall" (poem)	"Hallelujah Chorus" from The Messiah

Titles Without Underlining or Quotation Marks

Do not underline or place in quotation marks mentions of the Bible and other holy scriptures or their parts. No marking is required for titles of government charters, alliances, treaties, acts, statutes, or reports.

TITLES WITHOUT UNDERLINING OR QUOTATION MARKS
the Bible, the Koran (religious works)
Bill of Rights, Declaration of Independence (government documents)

EXERCISE A: Punctuating Different Types of Works. Use underlining or quotation marks with the works in each sentence. One item does not require punctuation.

EXAMPLE: The song Shall We Dance? comes from the musical The King and I.
The song "Shall We Dance?" comes from the musical The King and I.

1. The first book in the New Testament is Matthew.
2. We have just finished reading the Inferno from Dante's Divine Comedy.
3. The background music was The March of the Toys from Babes in Toyland.
4. Each evening the band on the Queen Elizabeth 2 played God Save the Queen.
5. Did you read the article The Land of the Dead in last week's Time?

EXERCISE B: Choosing the Correct Form. Circle the correct form in each item.

1. "Hamlet" or Hamlet
2. Genesis or Genesis
3. "Happy Birthday" or Happy Birthday
4. The Magna Carta or the Magna Carta
5. The "Nutcracker Suite" or the Nutcracker Suite

Dashes and Parentheses

Dashes

Use dashes to indicate an abrupt change of thought, a dramatic interrupting idea, or a summary statement. Use dashes to set off a nonessential appositive or parenthetical expression when it is long, when it is already punctuated, or when you want to be dramatic.

USES OF THE DASH	
Change of Thought	I'll be with you in a minute—oh, oh, there's the phone again.
Dramatic Interruption	That musical—the production numbers are spectacular—has been running on Broadway for years.
Summary Statement	Nuts, fruits, and grains—all are nutritious foods.
Nonessential Element	The woman who proposed the plan—a wealthy widow who owns two villas, a Manhattan townhouse, and a yacht—has always had liberal ideas. When Stacy saw the new car—can you believe this?—she fainted.

EXERCISE A: Using the Dash. Add dashes where they are needed in the following sentences.

EXAMPLE: Tanya's report Ms. Wilson raved about it was heavily documented.
   Tanya's report—Ms. Wilson raved about it—was heavily documented.

1. In the first presentation it was just an illusion, of course a small ball was passed through a solid mirror.
2. One of the exhibits you would have loved it depicted colonial baking in a hearth oven.
3. The justices of the Supreme Court, the complete Senate, and the members of the House of Representatives all assembled to hear the State of the Union message.
4. The librarian you know Mrs. Norman was very helpful in finding the information I needed.
5. I know I have that paper somewhere oh, never mind.
6. Whitney Jones an interesting man who has spent most of his life in Saudi Arabia is teaching a course at Rutgers this fall.
7. Don Mattingly, Dwight Gooden, Dave Winfield, Ron Guidry all are famous baseball players.
8. They are serving strawberry ice cream your favorite for dessert.
9. The storm seems to be over no, the sky is darkening again.
10. Joe Smith a golfer with a handicap of two is fifty years old.

EXERCISE B: More Work with Dashes. Follow the instructions for Exercise A.

1. Actors take particular pride in receiving major awards the Oscar for motion pictures, the Tony for Broadway plays, and the Emmy for television because they are chosen by their peers.
2. I wonder what could be keeping Elena hey, there's her car now.
3. Yesterday's football victory the crowd was ecstatic guarantees us a chance at the state title.
4. The woman I met at the museum I think her name was Barker or Barkus used to work with Mom at the bank.
5. Turkey, stuffing, cranberry sauce, pies all are traditional dishes for an American Thanksgiving dinner.

16.6 Dashes and Parentheses

Parentheses

Use parentheses to set off asides and explanations only when the material is not essential or when it consists of one or more sentences. Use parentheses to set off numbers or letters used with items in a series and with certain numerical references such as birth and death dates.

USES OF PARENTHESES	
Phrases	This gray sweater (old and baggy as it is) is my favorite.
Sentences	This summer my friend Marissa is coming for a visit. (She lives in Montana.) We have gone to the same camp for years.
Numbers or Letters	Mom left a list of specific chores: (1) make the beds, (2) set the table, and (3) make a salad.
Dates	The Magna Carta (1215 A.D.) established the right to trial by a jury of one's peers.

The chart below illustrates the rules for punctuating and capitalizing material in parentheses. Notice, too, the punctuation outside the parentheses.

CAPITALIZATION AND PUNCTUATION WITH PARENTHESES	
Declarative Sentence	When Joey cries (he's six months old) and wakes the whole family, we all try to remember we wanted a baby.
Interrogative or Exclamatory Sentence	After I finish my exercise class (Why did I ever sign up?), I am always exhausted.
Sentence Between Sentences	We placed the catalog order six weeks ago. (It was for fifty dollars worth of merchandise.) However, it still has not arrived.

EXERCISE A: Using Parentheses. Add parentheses wherever they are appropriate.

EXAMPLE: After the assassination of Julius Caesar 44 B.C., a triumvirate ruled Rome.
   After the assassination of Julius Caesar *(44 B.C.)*, a triumvirate ruled Rome.

1. As soon as we had finished dinner it was about 6:30, I started my homework.
2. We considered several plans for raising funds: a a bake sale, b a bottle drive, or c a plant sale.
3. In the Battle of Hastings 1066, William of Normandy defeated the English.
4. Jason's favorite pet he has several unusual ones is a boa constrictor.
5. Considering the distance between the two cities 3,124 miles, to be exact, driving seems impractical.

EXERCISE B: More Work with Parentheses. Rewrite each sentence, adding parentheses and capitalization where necessary.

EXAMPLE: Zach's jack-o-lantern smile he had lost his first tooth was cute.
   Zach's jack-o-lantern smile (he had lost his first tooth) was cute.

1. Beth's party what a wonderful party it was! lasted till midnight.

_____

2. Benjamin Franklin 1706–1790 was an extremely versatile man.

_____

16.7 Hyphens

Using Hyphens

Use a hyphen when writing out numbers from twenty-one through ninety-nine and with fractions used as adjectives. Also use hyphens with certain prefixes and compound words, with compound modifiers (except those ending with *-ly*) before nouns, and to avoid confusion.

USES OF HYPHENS	
With Numbers	twenty-eight flavors, one-fourth cup
With Prefixes	pro-American, self-conscious, ex-governor
With Compound Nouns	mother-in-law, passer-by, merry-go-round
With Compound Modifiers	best-dressed performer, well-manicured lawn, tie-dyed shirt, carefully maintained yard
For Clarity	re-fined versus refined, five-acre lots versus five acre-lots

Using Hyphens at the Ends of Lines

Divide words only between syllables. A word with a prefix or suffix can almost always be divided between the prefix and root or root and suffix. Divide a hyphenated word only after the hyphen. Do not divide a word so that only one letter stands alone. Do not divide proper nouns or adjectives, and do not carry part of a word over to another page.

HYPHENS AT THE ENDS OF LINES						
Correct	tho-rough	un-happy	ex-officer	de-part	ques-tion	English
Incorrect	thor-ough	unh-appy	ex-of-ficer	a-part	ver-y	Eng-lish

EXERCISE A: Using Hyphens. Place hyphens where they are needed. (Not all sentences need hyphens.)

EXAMPLE: Jeremy is an all around athlete.
         Jeremy is an all-around athlete.

1. The sergeant at arms asked the demonstrators to leave the meeting.
2. Alison's half hearted response disappointed us.
3. Of the twenty four bottles in the case, three were broken.
4. You will need five eighths yard of fabric for the sleeves alone.
5. Like many other commonly held beliefs, this one has no foundation.
6. Even as a young child, Paul was very self sufficient.
7. Several anti Iranian demonstrators were jailed.
8. That hand carved mantel is a masterpiece.
9. We will have several out of town guests with us for the holidays.
10. Twenty seven students in our school were nominated to the National Honor Society.

EXERCISE B: Hyphenating Words. Rewrite each word below, using a hyphen at any place where the word could be divided at the end of a line of writing.

EXAMPLE: amusing __*amus-ing*__   badge __*badge*__

1. misspell _____
2. Athenian _____
3. create _____
4. Scandinavian _____
5. above _____

16.8 Apostrophes

Apostrophes with Possessive Nouns

Use the following rules to form the possessives of nouns.

FORMING POSSESSIVE NOUNS	
Add an apostrophe and an -s to most singular nouns.	the cat's basket the scientist's experiment
Add just an apostrophe to plural nouns ending in -s.	the cats' paw print the scientists' discussions
Add an apostrophe and an -s to plural nouns that do not end in -s.	the women's jobs the mice's nest
Make the last word in a compound noun possessive.	the stage manager's clipboard the Girl Scouts' jamboree
Treat time, amounts, and the word *sake* like other possessives.	a moment's hesitation; ten cents' worth; for Ann's sake; for the Smiths' sake
To show individual ownership, make each noun in the series possessive.	Ted's, Jim's, and Cliff's bunks the boys' and girls' locker rooms
To show joint ownership, make the last noun in the series possessive.	Ted, Jim, and Cliff's room the boys and girls' teacher

Apostrophes with Pronouns

Use an apostrophe and an -s with indefinite pronouns to show possession. Do not use an apostrophe with possessive forms of personal pronouns, which are already possessive.

POSSESSIVE FORMS OF PRONOUNS		
Indefinite		**Personal**
either's	no one's	my, mine, our, ours
anybody's	one's	your, yours
someone's	each other's	his, her, hers, its, their, theirs

EXERCISE A: Writing Possessive Forms. Write the possessive form in the space provided.

EXAMPLE: the apples from that tree   _that tree's apples_

1. the toys of the children _____

2. salary for two weeks _____

3. the trunk on the elephant _____

4. the birthday of my sister-in-law _____

5. the apartment of Elinor and her sister _____

EXERCISE B: Using Apostrophes Correctly with Pronouns. Underline the correct pronoun in each set in parentheses.

EXAMPLE: The books on the end table must be (<u>yours</u>, your's).

1. Joyce found her sneakers in (their, they're) usual place in her locker.
2. This must be (someone elses', someone else's) notebook.
3. Ben and Andy both made suggestions; we could accept (neithers, neither's).
4. Shall we meet at your house or (ours, our's)?
5. It is (anyone's, anyones') guess who will win the election.

16.8 Apostrophes

Apostrophes with Contractions

Use an apostrophe in a contraction to indicate the position of the missing letter or letters. The most common contractions are those formed with verbs.

COMMON CONTRACTIONS			
Verbs with *Not*	isn't (is not)	can't (cannot)	won't (will not)
Pronouns with Verbs	I'll (I will) I'm (I am) I'd (I would) I've (I have)	you'll (you will) you're (you are) you'd (you would) you've (you have)	we'll (we will) they're (they are) he'd (he would) she's (she is)
Other Kinds of Contractions	o'clock C'mon	class of '85 comin'	

Special Uses of the Apostrophe

Use an apostrophe and an *-s* to write the plurals of numbers, symbols, letters, and words used to name themselves.

EXAMPLE: Dot your *i*'s and cross your *t*'s.
        Avoid using so many *and*'s.

EXERCISE A: Writing Contractions. Write contractions from the words in parentheses to complete each sentence.

EXAMPLE: _He's_   been working hard all day.   (He has)

1. _____ never seen a cow before.   (They had)

2. I wonder if _____ going to be late.   (we are)

3. Sandy always says _____ rather stay home.   (he would)

4. _____ been waiting for the bus for over an hour.   (We have)

5. Uncle Max says _____ his favorite nephew.   (I am)

6. Lorna replied that she _____ be able to join us.   (will not)

7. Len, _____ you going to eat with us?   (are not)

8. I must fix dinner tonight, if _____ not home.   (you are)

9. I hope _____ visit us again soon.   (you will)

10. I _____ heard from Ellen for several weeks.   (have not)

EXERCISE B: Using Apostrophes Correctly. Add one or more apostrophes to each of the following sentences.

EXAMPLE: The *s indicate items most sorely needed.
        The *'s indicate items most sorely needed.

1. Lou has a strange way of making his *g*s.

2. My father graduated in the class of 66.

3. The concert will begin promptly at eight oclock.

4. I cant tell your *e*s from your *i*s.

5. Michelle makes her 7s in the European style.

17.1 Prewriting

Exploring Ideas

To explore ideas for writing topics, take inventory of your interests, experiences, and ideas.

TECHNIQUES FOR GENERATING IDEAS	
Interviewing Yourself	Ask yourself questions to discover topics that interest you.
Free Writing	Write anything that comes into your mind.
Journal Writing	Keep a daily record of your thoughts, feelings, and experiences.
Reading and Saving	Read as much and as often as possible.
Clustering	Think of words associated with a chosen topic.
Brainstorming	Start with any idea and build on it, trying to go in as many directions as possible.
Cueing	Use a variety of devices to stimulate ideas.

Choosing and Narrowing a Topic

Choose a topic that can be effectively covered in the allotted amount of space.

EXERCISE A: Interviewing Yourself. Answer the questions below to help you generate ideas for potential writing topics.

1. What activities do you enjoy? _____

   _____

2. What events have happened to you in the past that have made you frightened, glad, or wiser? _____

   _____

3. What events would you like to have happen to you in the future? _____

   _____

4. What books, articles, or movies have made an impression on you, and why? _____

   _____

5. What people do you know whose lives and/or stories interest you? _____

   _____

   _____

EXERCISE B: Free Writing. On a separate piece of paper, write for ten minutes, nonstop, on one of the following topics. Don't worry about spelling or punctuation. Just keep writing. Start with general reactions and move to specific ones. Include any sights, sounds, or other details associated with the subject.

moving to a new place	your favorite book
losing an important game	going to a foreign country
losing a close friend	flying in a jet
approaching a boy or girl you like	growing up
the end of summer	walking through a rainstorm
your favorite rock group	learning an important lesson

17.1 Prewriting

Determining Audience and Purpose

Determine your audience and purpose before you begin writing.

Developing a Main Idea and Support

State a main idea. Then gather and organize supporting information to develop the main idea effectively.

ORGANIZATION OF SUPPORTING INFORMATION	
Chronological Order	Information arranged in time sequence
Spatial Order	Information arranged according to space relationships
Order of Importance	Information arranged from least to most important or vice versa
Comparison and Contrast	Information arranged according to similarities and differences between items
Development	Information arranged so that one point leads logically to the next point

EXERCISE A: Determining Audience and Purpose. Choose one of the five broad topics below. Then complete the work that follows.

politics   history   music   theater   sports

1. Use the clustering technique to narrow the topic you have chosen into one that is narrow enough to be covered in a short paper. Then write your topic. _____

_____

2. Write a possible purpose for your paper. _____

_____

3. Write another possible purpose for your paper. _____

_____

4. Identify a potential audience for the purpose you wrote in #2. _____

_____

5. Identify a potential audience for the purpose you wrote in #3. _____

_____

EXERCISE B: Developing a Topic. Complete the work below to develop your topic from Exercise A.

1. Decide on your main idea. _____

_____

2. Make a list of supporting information. _____

_____

_____

_____

3. Choose a method for organizing the information you wrote in #2. _____

_____

4. Arrange your information according to the method you chose in #3. _____

_____

_____

17.2 Writing

Writing a First Draft

Translate your prewriting notes into sentences and paragraphs, without worrying about punctuation, spelling, grammar, or perfect sentences. While you are writing, you may want to rework your ideas, change your approach, or even change your entire topic.

SAMPLE ROUGH DRAFT

Martha's Vineyard is a small island off the coast of Massachusetts. It is a popular vacation spot, and its popularity has been growing in recent years. One reason for the island's growth in popularity is its secluded nature. Islanders have taken steps to limit development so that the island can retain a secluded, New England coastal flavor. Another reason for the island's popularity is the diversity of its villages. There are six towns on the island, and each town has its own character. There are also many beautiful beaches on the island that are a major attraction for tourists. Because of the island's beauty, diversity, and secluded character it has become one of the most popular vacation spots in the Northeast.

Overcoming Writer's Block

Use prewriting techniques, such as free writing, reading and saving, and brainstorming to help you overcome writer's block.

EXERCISE A: Writing a First Draft. Choose one of the topics below. Then write a paragraph based on the prewriting information that follows. Feel free to rework the ideas that are presented below as you are writing, and do not hesitate to use some of your own ideas to assist you in developing your paragraph.

Topics:	school government	rock music	the value of college
Purposes:	to inform	to entertain	to persuade
Audiences:	your classmates	young people	high school students
Order:	developmental	chronological	order of importance
Supporting Information:	1. so students have input into how school is run 2. to bring about change 3. modeled after U.S. system 4. gives students better idea of how government works	1. started in 1950's 2. gained more popularity with the Beatles in 1960's 3. during 1970's new technology affected sound 4. 1980's return to more basic sound, like the 1950's	1. gives people advantage in job market 2. allows people to learn by taking a wide variety of courses 3. provides a wide variety of extracurricular activities 4. students grow through experience

EXERCISE B: More Work with First Drafts. On separate paper, write a first draft based on the prewriting activities that you completed in Exercises A and B on page 113. Do not worry about grammar, spelling, or punctuation. Just get your thoughts down on paper. Once you have finished, save your paper so that you can work on revising it.

17.3 Revising

Revising for Sense

Make sure that all of the ideas in a paper support your purpose and that they are presented in a logical way with clearly perceivable connections between them.

REVISING FOR SENSE
1. Make sure that you have clearly stated your topic.
2. Make sure that your main idea will be clear to your readers.
3. Make sure that there is enough relevant supporting information.
4. Make sure that your ideas are presented in a logical order.
5. Make sure that the logical connections between ideas have been expressed.

Editing for Word Choice and Sentences

Read your paper several times, making sure that every word is the best possible one to express your thoughts and that your sentences are clear and varied.

EDITING WORDS AND SENTENCES
1. Make sure that each word conveys the meaning that you intended it to.
2. Make sure that the language is appropriate for the intended audience.
3. Make sure that the meaning of each sentence is clear.
4. Make sure that you have varied the lengths and structures of your sentences.

Proofreading and Publishing

Proofreading involves making final corrections in spelling, capitalization, punctuation, and grammar. Once you have your final version, decide on the best way to distribute it to your intended audience.

EXERCISE A: Revising and Editing a Paper. Revise and edit the paper you wrote in Exercise B on page 114 by answering the questions below and by making appropriate changes when your response to a question is *no.*

1. Have you made your topic and main idea clear to your readers? _____

2. Is there enough relevant supporting information and is it presented clearly? _____

3. Does each word in your paper convey the meaning that you intended it to? _____

4. Is the language appropriate for the intended audience, and is the meaning of each sentence clear? _____

5. Have you varied the lengths and structures of your sentences? _____

EXERCISE B: Proofreading a Paper. Proofread the paper you revised in Exercise A, correcting any errors in grammar, spelling, punctuation, and capitalization. Then recopy your paper neatly and think of how you want to present it to your audience.

18.1 Choosing Precise Words

Using Action Words

Use action verbs and verbs in the active voice to make your writing more precise.

Linking Verbs	Action Verbs
The Falcons *were* the losers in their opening game. Each event *was* a test of a different skill.	The Falcons *lost* their opening game. Each event *tested* a different skill.
Passive Voice	**Active Voice**
The fort *was captured* by the enemy. Our house *was sold* in only three days.	The enemy *captured* the fort. We *sold* our house in only three days.

Using Specific Words

Use specific verbs, nouns, and adjectives to make your meaning precise.

General Words	Specific Words
The campers *talked* in the darkness. Ellen is studying physics in *school*. The clock is *old* and *valuable*.	The campers *chattered* in the darkness. Ellen is studying physics in *college*. That clock is a *priceless antique*.

EXERCISE A: Using Action Words. Rewrite each sentence, replacing the vague or imprecise verb with an action verb in the active voice.

EXAMPLE: Alan's attitude may be a hindrance to our progress.
       Alan's attitude may hinder our progress.

1. Mr. Perkins was sent for by the principal.

_____

2. Ellison was a more aggressive campaigner than Perkins.

_____

3. Jenny's plan was a proposal to revise the dress code.

_____

4. The house next door was bought by a family from Idaho.

_____

5. The child's insolence was an embarrassment to his parents.

_____

EXERCISE B: Replacing General Words. On the line after each sentence write a more exact word or expression to replace the underlined word.

EXAMPLE: The police car <u>went</u> through the intersection.   *sped*

1. The defense attorney <u>presented</u> the case forcefully. _____

2. The day was perfect for a <u>walk</u> through the woods. _____

3. The candidate's ignorance of the facts <u>surprised</u> us. _____

4. A <u>party</u> will mark the theater's twenty-fifth anniversary. _____

5. That restaurant serves <u>good</u> food. _____

18.1 Choosing Precise Words

Using Vivid Words

Replace clichés with specific words that clearly express your meaning. Write your own similes and metaphors to sharpen your ideas and impressions.

Clichés and Dead Metaphors	Fresh, Clear Expressions
Frustrated with her piano practice, Elsa *threw in the towel*.	Frustrated with her piano practice, Elsa *banged the keyboard like a carpenter driving in the last nail*.
Phil has *bitten off more than he can chew*.	Phil has *undertaken a larger job than he can handle*.

Using Varied Words

Avoid careless overuse of the same word. Replace obvious and unnecessary modifiers with modifiers that are more precise and vivid or with specific details.

Overused Words	Varied Words
The *laughing* baby *laughed* and waved her arms.	The *laughing* baby *gurgled* and waved her arms.
Sheep grazed on the *green grass*.	Sheep grazed in the *lush pasture*.

EXERCISE A: Eliminating Clichés and Dead Metaphors. Rewrite each sentence, replacing clichés and dead metaphors with original expressions.

EXAMPLE: Phoebe's comments always get right to the heart of the matter.
          Phoebe's comments always express the main point clearly.

1. Dan is in the doghouse for taking the car without permission.

   _____

2. At large parties, I am often at a loss for words.

   _____

3. It goes without saying that Donna will be elected class president.

   _____

4. Fran felt like a fish out of water at the formal reception.

   _____

5. When the chips are down, I can always count on Pete.

   _____

EXERCISE B: Eliminating Careless Repetition and Obvious Modifiers. Underline an unnecessary repetition or obvious modifier in each sentence. On the line at the right, write a vivid modifier or precise word to replace the underlined word.

EXAMPLE: Many tourists visit the large mansion daily. *sprawling*

1. That painter paints only landscapes. _____

2. Few forms of life survive in the sandy desert. _____

3. For most of the day we drove past rural farmlands. _____

4. The tall mountains were reflected on the surface of the lake. _____

5. The builders built the new porch in three weeks. _____

18.2 Maintaining an Appropriate Tone

Understanding the Ingredients of Tone

Consider your audience, subject, and purpose to determine the tone for a piece of writing.

POSSIBLE TONES WRITING CAN HAVE			
aloof	confidential	indifferent	playful
angry	conversational	informal	pretentious
calm	emotional	ironic	scholarly
casual	familiar	light	sentimental
chatty	formal	matter-of-fact	serious
coaxing	humorous	nostalgic	solemn
condescending	impersonal	objective	somber

Avoiding Inappropriate Words

Replace slang words with words that are suitable for your estabished tone. Replace jargon with words that are appropriate for your specific audience. Replace self-important language with simpler, more direct words. Avoid an insincere tone in your writing by removing euphemisms from your sentences. Replace overly emotional language with reasonable words that are more neutral.

EXERCISE A: Identifying Tone. Identify the tone of each item below by writing two or three terms from the chart above.

EXAMPLE: Given the current data, the outcome of the disease is difficult to predict.
formal, impersonal, matter-of-fact

1. Come on, all you movie lovers! Make your reservations now for the first annual Hollywood Nostalgia Night! _____

2. From textual clues alone, we can determine the author's interest in American culture. External biographical evidence supports the theory even further. _____

3. Anyone who cares about the future of the planet, anyone who loves animals, anyone who recognizes the beauty of nature must support the proposal. _____

4. After you have finished your sail, maybe you'd like to come over to our boat for a light supper. We'd enjoy spending some more time with you. _____

5. Despite numerous overtures to increase participation, overall productivity in the organization has diminished markedly. _____

EXERCISE B: Avoiding Inappropriate Words. Underline any inappropriate words in each sentence. Then write an appropriate replacement for the underlined word or words on the line at the right.

EXAMPLE: Standby ticket holders will be boarded <u>in accordance with</u>
the regulations stated on each ticket. _according to_

1. My English teacher is a really mellow dude. _____

2. Students should strive to maximize their utilization of time. _____

3. When I was young I fell out of a tree and cracked my cranium.

_____

4. Most of the other faculty members feel that professor Hawkins is too laid back.

_____

5. Mrs. Smith will not tolerate any freeloaders in her boarding house.

_____

18.3 Using Words Concisely

Eliminating Deadwood

Eliminate hedging words and empty words from your sentences.

RECOGNIZING DEADWOOD	
Hedging Words	**Empty Words**
it seems that	it is a fact that
quite	it is also true that
somewhat	as I said before
rather	on account of the fact that
almost	despite the fact that
kind of	the reason was because
sort of	the area of
tends to	the thing is
it is my opinion that	to the extent that
in my opinion	needless to say
I think that	by way of

Avoiding Redundancy

Eliminate redundant words, phrases, and clauses from your sentences.

Redundant	Concise
The *wet* water was refreshing.	The water was refreshing.
It was an unforgettable day *that no one will be able to forget*.	It was an unforgettable day.

Avoiding Wordiness

Reduce a wordy clause or phrase to a shorter structure or to a single word.

Wordy	Concise
Wendy became a mother *to the lost boys*.	Wendy became the *lost boys'* mother.
Ed limped in *in an awkward way*.	Ed limped in *awkwardly*.

EXERCISE A: Recognizing Deadwood, Redundancy, and Wordiness. In each sentence below, cross out any empty or hedging words. Underline any instance of redundancy or wordiness.

EXAMPLE: I inherited the cameo <u>that had belonged to my mother</u>.

1. It is my opinion that a springtime plant sale in the spring is a good way to raise funds.
2. My brother, who is older than I am, joined the Navy.
3. The cold ice quickly melted in the hot water.
4. Tom and Bill could not move the piano, which was heavy.
5. It is my personal belief that I have studied long enough.

EXERCISE B: Avoiding Deadwood, Redundancy, and Wordiness. Rewrite each sentence in Exercise A to make it more concise.

EXAMPLE: *I inherited my mother's cameo.*

1. _____
2. _____
3. _____
4. _____
5. _____

19.1 Sentence Combining

Combining Ideas

Join two or more short sentences by using compound subjects or verbs, by using phrases, or by writing compound, complex, or compound-complex sentences.

Separate Sentences	Combined Sentences
Westfield won its game last night. Branford also won.	*Westfield and Branford* won their games last night.
The boy screamed for his mother. He realized that he was lost.	*Realizing that he was lost,* the boy screamed for his mother.
The firemen battled to control the fire. It continued to spread. The wind had shifted directions.	The firemen battled to control the fire, *but* it continued to spread *because* the wind had shifted directions.

EXERCISE A: Combining Sentences. Combine the sentences in each item into a single, longer sentence.

EXAMPLE: Al refused to accompany us to the top of the Empire State Building. He is terrified of high places.
      Because he is terrified of high places, Al refused to accompany us to the top of the Empire State Building.

1. Broadway musicals are often difficult for amateurs. They have large casts and elaborate production numbers. _____

   _____

2. My favorite breakfast is pancakes. I like to have bacon with my pancakes. _____

   _____

3. It is a quality magazine. It is intended for people interested in science. _____

   _____

4. Timmy made the birdhouse himself. He just followed the directions. _____

   _____

5. Today's editorial was quite alarming. It was about toxic waste. _____

   _____

EXERCISE B: More Work with Combining Sentences. Follow the directions in Exercise A.

1. He is a very gifted athlete. He works hard in practice. He is the best player on the team. _____

   _____

2. The band members wanted to leave the stage. The crowd implored them to continue. They played another song. _____

   _____

3. Gerri's children were grown. She went back to school. She became a physical therapist. _____

   _____

4. Sean never does well on standardized tests. He gets good grades in school. He works very hard.

   _____

5. The ice storm lasted for two days. The roads were treacherous. School was canceled for the week.

   _____

19.2 Varying Your Sentences

Expanding Short Sentences

Expand short sentences by adding details.

Short Sentences	Expanded Sentences
The boy swam across the lake. The girl studied all night.	The *young* boy *easily* swam across the *large* lake. The girl, *Wendy Smith, an excellent student,* studied all night.

Shortening Long Sentences

Break up lengthy, overly complicated sentences into simpler, shorter sentences.

Long, Complicated Sentence	Shorter, Clearer Sentences
The essay contest, which was announced last week by the Chamber of Commerce, appealed to many of us in the Scribblers' Club, particularly because of the cash prize, but many of us were reluctant to enter because of the early deadline, which would conflict with studying for final exams.	The Chamber of Commerce essay contest announced last week appealed to many of us in the Scribblers' Club. The cash prize was particularly appealing. However, the conflict between studying for final exams and meeting the early deadline made many of us reluctant to enter.

EXERCISE A: Adding Details to Short Sentences. Improve each of the following sentences by adding the item or items in parentheses.

EXAMPLE: The player won the tournament. (Two adjectives)
         The *best* player won the *tennis* tournament.

1. Jody speaks French fluently.   (Appositive phrase) _____

   _____

2. The guitarist broke a string.   (Prepositional phrase) _____

   _____

3. Jane skied to the bottom of the hill.   (Two adverbs) _____

   _____

4. Senator Williams came to our school.   (Verbal phrase) _____

   _____

5. The soldiers marched across the field.   (Two adjectives) _____

   _____

EXERCISE B: Shortening Long Sentences. Divide the sentence below into two or more sentences.

Although the doctors had not held out much hope for the surgery, the family remained optimistic throughout the long hours of the operation, thinking that if they wanted it badly enough surely things would work out, and they were ecstatic when the surgeon appeared and reported that the operation had indeed been a success.

_____

_____

_____

_____

19.2 Varying Your Sentences

Using Different Sentence Openers and Structures

Use a variety of sentence openers and structures.

VARIED SENTENCE OPENERS	
Modifier First	*Carefully*, the detective put the evidence into the bag.
Phrase First	*Looking down from the mountain*, we saw the winding river.
Clause First	*Whenever Grandma visits us*, she bakes an applesauce cake.

Monotonous Sentences	Varied Sentences
My sister is a doctor. She went to college for four years. She spent four years in medical school. She has spent three years in residency. She will finish this summer. She will go into private practice. She specialized in internal medicine.	My sister, who is a doctor, spent four years in medical school, after her four years of college. When she finishes her three-year residency this summer, she will go into private practice in internal medicine.

EXERCISE A: Using Different Sentence Openers. Rewrite each sentence to make it begin with a one-word modifier, a phrase, or a clause.

EXAMPLE: Alison sometimes baby-sits for her cousins.
                  Sometimes, Alison baby-sits for her cousins.

1. Phone the box office for further information.

   _____

2. The youngsters were especially excited about their trip because they had never been camping before.

   _____

3. Can you join us for a pizza after the game?

   _____

4. Uncle John frequently dozes off after dinner.

   _____

5. The band members will have a bake sale to raise money for their trip.

   _____

EXERCISE B: Varying Sentence Structures. Rewrite the following paragraph, using a variety of sentence structures.

   (1) Jeremy wants to be a veterinarian.   (2) He has loved animals all his life.   (3) He had a whole menagerie of pets as a child.   (4) He took excellent care of them.   (5) He never could bear to see an animal suffer.   (6) He nursed several injured chipmunks and other small animals back to health.
(7) He has always been a good student.   (8) He has done especially well in math and science.
(9) He will graduate from high school this June.   (10) He plans to take pre-med courses at college this fall.

   _____

   _____

   _____

   _____

   _____

19.2 Varying Your Sentences

Using Special Sentence Patterns

Use parallelism to underscore ideas. Use a new structure after a series of similar structures to underscore an idea.

SPECIAL SENTENCE PATTERNS	
Parallel Structures	In store windows, in the buildings on the town green, and in private homes, a single candle burned in each window. Jackson would tax the rich and the corporations; Hillyer would tax the poor and the small businesses.
Breaking a Pattern	I have studied the manual; I have assembled the materials; I have set up a work space. Now wish me luck!

EXERCISE A: Using Parallelism. Each sentence below contains an element that is not parallel to others. Rewrite each one using parallel structures.

EXAMPLE: We were hungry and cold but not feeling tired.
            We were hungry and cold but not tired.

1. Sewing, painting, and to cook gourmet meals are Alice's hobbies.

   _____

2. Hank explained his idea clearly, completely, and with patience.

   _____

3. Jamie agreed to work at night and on weekends but not holidays.

   _____

4. Clapping hands, stamping feet, and with loud whistles, the audience demanded an encore.

   _____

5. Fran likes to swim and to sail but not playing baseball.

   _____

EXERCISE B: Using Special Sentence Patterns. Follow the instructions to write sentences that make good use of parallel structures.

EXAMPLE: Write two parallel clauses that emphasize a contrast.
            Ramon is reflective and deliberate; Jed is impulsive and spontaneous.

1. Write a sentence with three parallel prepositional phrases that emphasize thoroughness.

   _____

2. Write two parallel clauses that emphasize similarity.

   _____

3. Write two parallel clauses that emphasize a contrast.

   _____

4. Set up a pattern with three similar sentences. Then break the pattern to emphasize a final point in the fourth sentence.

   _____

   _____

   _____

   _____

19.3 Making Clear Connections

Using Transitions

Use transitions logically to clarify the relationship between ideas in different sentences.

USEFUL TRANSITIONS		
Time	**Comparison/Contrast**	
after before earlier first meantime next	indeed however nevertheless on the other hand	
Cause/Effect	**Addition/Examples**	**Emphasis**
as a result then consequently therefore	for example namely furthermore that is	indeed in other words in fact thus

Using Coordination and Subordination

Use coordination logically to join equal and related words, phrases, and clauses within a sentence. Use subordination logically to connect related but unequal ideas in a single sentence.

Coordination	Subordination
New Hampshire is known for its colorful mountains and lakes; Maine is noted for its jagged but beautiful coastline.	Before you leave the house, button your coat. My bedroom, which is painted yellow, is very cheerful.

EXERCISE A: Using Transitions. Improve each pair of sentences by adding the kind of transition indicated in parentheses.

EXAMPLE: Lightning struck the power line. The area was blacked out.   (effect)
Lightning struck the power line. As a result, the area was blacked out.

1. Anita always has good fund-raising ideas. She thought of the plant sale.   (example)

   _____

2. Hall is the only responsible candidate. There is no other choice.   (emphasis)

   _____

3. The governor is back at the state capital. She spoke at our school.   (time)

   _____

4. The new star is extremely talented. She is attractive.   (addition)

   _____

EXERCISE B: Using Coordination and Subordination. Turn each item into one sentence using the method given in parentheses.

EXAMPLE: Peter was late for dinner. His mother was very angry.   (coordination)
Peter was late for dinner; consequently, his mother was very angry.

1. Many people volunteered. Few actually worked.   (coordination)

   _____

2. We left for our trip. We made sure the house was in order.   (subordination)

   _____

3. Louise was depressed. Good music improved her mood.   (subordination)

   _____

4. Gail studied hard for her math test. She failed.   (coordination)

   _____

19.3 Making Clear Connections

Using Logical Order

Order your ideas logically and consistently within sentences and within groups of sentences

Illogical Order	Logical Order
The wind became gusty; huge drops began to fall; storm clouds gathered.	The wind became gusty; storm clouds gathered; huge drops began to fall.
The twins are excellent students. However, Moira does better in languages. Both do well in math and science.	The twins are excellent students. Both do well in math and science. However, Moira does better in languages.

EXERCISE A: Using Logical Order. If an item below is written in logical order, write *logical* on your paper. If an item is in illogical order, rewrite it to follow logical order.

EXAMPLE: Soon only a few scraps of paper were left in the house. The movers began carrying out the cartons and barrels. A huge van pulled up in front.

  A huge van pulled up in front. The movers began carrying out the cartons and barrels.
  Soon only a few scraps of paper were left in the house.

1. The last I saw, he was pedaling away from the house. Tom resented our parents' criticism. He stormed out of the house and slammed the door.

   _____

   _____

2. The prosecutor called the witness, the bailiff swore her in, and the questioning began.

   _____

3. The front of the house was impressive. A sunken living room went off to the right. Inside, a spiral staircase dominated the entryway.

   _____

   _____

4. Behind the band came the scout troops. A man dressed as Uncle Sam led off the parade.

   _____

5. Angie set the date, made up the guest list, and ordered the invitations.

   _____

EXERCISE B: Using Logical Order in a Paragraph. Rewrite the following paragraph, using a logical order for the sentences.

  (1) After unpacking the food and sharing the photo albums, we organized a softball game.   (2) We all met at the park at noon.   (3) We parted with promises to make this an annual event.   (4) The day of the family reunion finally arrived.   (5) Dinner was a pleasure, each branch of the family having brought a different dish.

_____

_____

_____

_____

_____

20.1 Understanding Paragraphs

Topic Sentences

The topic sentence expresses the main idea of a paragraph.

POSITIONS FOR TOPIC SENTENCES	
Beginning	To give a sense of direction to the whole paragraph
Middle	To give a sense of direction to the paragraph after a short introductory sentence or two
End	To act as a summary of the whole paragraph

Support

Examples, details, facts, reasons, and incidents support the topic sentence.

KINDS OF SUPPORTING INFORMATION	
Examples	Specific instances of a more general statement
Details	Pieces of information that help describe something
Facts	True statements that offer useful information
Reasons	Arguments that help persuade
Incidents	Events that explain or tell a story

EXERCISE A: Examining a Paragraph. Read the following paragraph. Then answer the questions that appear below it.

(1) The guidance counselor had encouraged Beth to pursue her desire to become a physical therapist. (2) Her aptitude tests had confirmed her interest in science. (3) They had also showed that she would work well with people. (4) Physical therapy would also involve Beth's other special interests. (5) Her athletic ability and knowledge of anatomy, for instance, would be additional assets. (6) Everything seemed to confirm Beth's original career choice.

1. Which sentence acts as the topic sentence? _____

2. What purpose does the topic sentence serve? _____

3. Which sentences offer supporting information? _____

4. Which sentences offer reasons? _____

5. Which sentence gives examples? _____

EXERCISE B: Developing Support for Topic Sentences. Read each of the following topic sentences. Then tell what kind of support you would emphasize most in each paragraph. (Use each kind of support only once.)

EXAMPLE: The team has acquired a number of promising new players. _examples_

1. The appearance of the house supports the theory that it is haunted. _____

2. The new town charter will improve the government's efficiency. _____

3. Current government statistics show an increase in jobs in electronics. _____

4. The new shopping mall offers something for every taste and pocketbook. _____

5. Our trip to Williamsburg included some unexpected events. _____

20.1 Understanding Paragraphs

Unity

A paragraph is unified if all of its sentences illustrate and develop the topic sentence. Remove any sentences that are not closely related.

Lack of Unity	Unity
During the sixties, music was used by the younger generation as a means for expressing its desire for change. *Young people had long hair. They went to concerts wearing flowers in their hair. Some had peace signs embroidered onto their jackets.* Many songs dealt with American involvement in the war in Vietnam—one of the central causes of the young people's discontent.	During the sixties, music was used by the younger generation as a means for expressing its desire for change. Song lyrics focused on certain aspects and manifestations of society that a large proportion of young people found distasteful. Many songs dealt with American involvement in the war in Vietnam—one of the central causes of the young people's discontent.

Coherence

A paragraph is coherent if all the sentences are ordered logically and connected clearly. Also helping to achieve coherence are repetition of main words and synonyms and a concluding sentence.

ELEMENTS OF COHERENCE	
Logical Order	chronological, spatial, order of importance, comparison and contrast, developmental
Transitions	first, above, most important, on the other hand
Main Words and Synonyms	story, narrative, tale
Concluding Sentence	The result is a compelling and memorable tale.

EXERCISE A: Recognizing Unity in a Paragraph. Read the following paragraph. Then answer the questions that appear below it.

(1) On our first visit to the new house, all we could see were the flaws. (2) Several screens on the front porch hung askew and displayed large holes. (3) Inside, the living room floor was marred and badly needed sanding. (4) The kitchen looked odd with no appliances, and the sink was marked with huge rust stains. (5) Many people prefer stainless steel sinks to enamel ones. (6) Upstairs, the hallway carpeting, which was a ghastly color, was snagged and soiled. (7) What's more, the bedrooms looked tiny without any furniture. (8) I have bunk beds for my room. (9) We all agreed, however, that for all its flaws the place had charm. (10) We knew that with a little hard work we could soon make the house a comfortable home.

1. Which sentence is the topic sentence? _____

2. Which sentences support the topic sentence? _____

3. Which sentences should be removed? _____

4. Why should the sentences you identified in Question #3 be removed? _____

EXERCISE B: Identifying Elements of Coherence. Reread the paragraph above, mentally removing the sentences that do not belong. Then answer the following questions.

1. What order is used in the paragraph? _____

2. What transitional words or phrases are used in the paragraph? _____

_____

3. What is one main word used twice in the paragraph? _____

4. What synonyms or closely related words are used for this word? _____

5. Which sentence, if any, serves as a concluding sentence? _____

20.1 Understanding Paragraphs

Special Kinds of Paragraphs

Special paragraphs differ from standard paragraphs but are still unified and logical. Special paragraphs may have an implied rather than stated topic sentence or may consist of only one or two sentences. They usually work with standard paragraphs in a longer piece of writing, sometimes serving as an introduction to, or a transition between standard paragraphs.

KINDS OF SPECIAL PARAGRAPHS	
Kind	**Purpose**
Introductory	to create a mood; to present background information
Transitional	to present additional details in support of the preceding paragraph; to comment on or interpret information clearly relating to the topic of the essay
Concluding	to act as a clincher for the entire piece of writing

EXERCISE A: Identifying Special Paragraphs. Read the following composition. Then identify each paragraph as *standard* or *special*.

(1) Picture this scene: Two-year-old Susie sits calmly in the yard stuffing berries of unknown origin into her mouth. Or try this one: Three-year-old Tommy lies under his bed screaming, "I hate you! I want my mom!" for two hours. Then he beams at you angelically when mom returns and asks, "Was everything all right?"

(2) There is no question that baby-sitting can be much more demanding than it appears to be on the surface. Sitters must remain calm and act quickly in an emergency. They must be able to soothe, calm, and cajole a frightened or stubborn youngster. They must be playmates, storytellers, and disciplinarians. They must, in fact, be substitute parents.

(3) Not all teenagers are prepared for the responsibilities of baby-sitting. Some expect to be able to study, chat on the phone, watch television, raid the refrigerator, or even entertain friends and be paid for the inconvenience of doing it in someone else's home. The realities of the job may suddenly appear in shocking contrast to their expectations.

(4) Spilled milk and far-flung peas horrify them. The pleas for "one more story" are often a prelude to a pillow fight that will try their patience. And the sobs from a nightmare only bewilder them.

(5) So think twice before you agree to sit for your neighbor's "little darlings." You must always be prepared to accept the responsibility that comes with this sort of job.

1. _____   3. _____   5. _____

2. _____   4. _____

EXERCISE B: Recognizing Different Kinds of Special Paragraphs. Below, write the number of each special paragraph you identified above. Then tell what kind of paragraph it is.

1. _____

2. _____

3. _____

20.4 Writing a Paragraph

Prewriting

1. Write your topic on the line below. Be sure it is narrow enough to be managed in a single paragraph.

TOPIC: _____

2. Now write your audience. Make one up if you don't have a real one.

AUDIENCE: _____

3. Next write your main idea. What would your audience want to know about the topic?

MAIN IDEA: _____

4. Now state your purpose (to inform, persuade, describe, or tell a story).

PURPOSE: _____

5. Next write a topic sentence that states your main idea in a way that is appropriate for your audience and purpose. (Try out a few before writing one below.)

TOPIC SENTENCE: _____

6. On a separate piece of paper, brainstorm for support. What questions might your audience have about your topic sentence? The answers are your support.

7. Look at your page of support. Cross out any items that are not necessary.

8. Now choose an order for your paragraph (chronological, spatial, order of importance, comparison and contrast, or developmental).

ORDER: _____

9. On a separate piece of paper outline your paragraph. Start with your topic sentence, and then organize your support according to the order you have chosen.

Writing

Using your outline, write your paragraph. Look for places to use transitions, repetitions of main words, synonyms, pronouns, and possibly parallelism; but don't worry about making everything perfect. This is just the first draft.

Revising

Write *yes* or *no* to each of the following questions. Then rework your first draft to fix all the items marked *no*.

1. Does the topic sentence clearly express the main idea of the paragraph? _____

2. Does the paragraph contain enough support to develop the topic sentence? _____

3. Is all of the supporting information appropriate? _____

4. Does the paragraph stick to the main idea? _____

5. Is the support presented in the most logical order? _____

6. Are there enough transitions, repetitions, and synonyms to connect the ideas? _____

7. Is a concluding sentence needed to wrap up the ideas? _____

8. Does the paragraph achieve its purpose? _____ Does it suit the audience? _____

9. Is every passage smooth and clear? _____

After you have improved your paragraph by turning the *no's* into *yes's*, **proofread** it carefully, looking for errors in grammar, mechanics, and spelling. If necessary, make a final copy and **proofread** it again.

21.1 Expository and Persuasive Writing

Expository Writing

The purpose of expository writing is to explain by setting forth information. Concentrate on explaining your main idea logically and fully.

ITEMS TO CONSIDER WHEN WRITING AN EXPOSITORY PARAGRAPH	
Topic Sentence	Make sure it is a direct factual statement.
Support	Make sure it is complete and logically arranged.
Language	Use clear, simple, direct language.

Persuasive Writing

The purpose of persuasive writing is to obtain the reader's agreement on a matter of opinion. Concentrate on influencing your audience.

ITEMS TO CONSIDER WHEN WRITING A PERSUASIVE PARAGRAPH	
Topic Sentence	Make sure it is a reasonable opinion on a significant topic.
Support	Use strong evidence and try to cover all arguments.
Language	Use reasonable language and try not to offend anyone.

EXERCISE A: Planning an Expository Paragraph. Circle one of the topics below. Then complete the prewriting activities that follow.

How marionettes work   The jogging craze   Discount stores and boutiques
How words change meaning   The pleasure of gardening   Gourmet food

1. Identify your audience. _____

2. Write a topic sentence. _____

3. Write three supporting ideas. _____

_____

4. Define or explain one technical term. _____

_____

5. Tell the order you would use. _____

EXERCISE B: Planning a Persuasive Paragraph. Circle one of the topics below. Then complete the prewriting activities that follow it.

Water fluoridation   Fast-food restaurants   Vegetarianism
Living in a big city   Required Latin courses   "Honesty is the best policy"

1. Identify your audience. _____

2. Write a topic sentence. _____

_____

3. Write two objections that might be raised by people who disagree with you. _____

_____

4. List three arguments you might use in your paragraph. _____

_____

_____

5. Tell the order you would use. _____

21.2 Descriptive and Narrative Writing

Descriptive Writing

Descriptive writing conveys a dominant impression through specific details, sensory impressions, and figures of speech. Concentrate on making your paragraphs as vivid as possible.

ITEMS TO CONSIDER WHEN WRITING A DESCRIPTIVE PARAGRAPH	
Topic Sentence	Use it to present a dominant impression.
Support	Try to include as many specific details as possible.
Language	Make your language colorful, use sensory impressions, and include any figures of speech that seem useful.

Narrative Writing

Narrative writing relates a chronological series of events from a single point of view. Concentrate on presenting a clear sequence of events.

ITEMS TO CONSIDER WHEN WRITING A NARRATIVE PARAGRAPH	
Topic Sentence	Use it to present a general truth or to set the scene.
Support	Organize it chronologically and maintain a consistent point of view.
Language	Use strong action verbs, colorful language, sensory impressions, and possibly a few figures of speech.

EXERCISE A: Planning a Descriptive Paragraph. Circle one of the topics below. Then complete the prewriting activities that follow.

> Michael Jackson   A holiday dinner table   A greenhouse
> A garage sale   A pirate's treasure chest   A muddy road

1. Identify your audience. _____

2. Write a topic sentence. _____

   _____

3. List three specific details. _____

   _____

4. List one sensory impression and one figure of speech you might use. _____

   _____

   _____

5. Tell the order you would use. _____

EXERCISE B: Planning a Narrative Paragraph. Circle one of the topics below. Then complete the prewriting activities that follow.

> Alone in a new place   A surprise party   A close call
> Clearing the air   The longest day   Being one's own worst enemy

1. Identify your audience. _____

2. Write a topic sentence. _____

   _____

3. List three events you would use. _____

   _____

4. Tell what point of view you would use. _____

5. List one action verb and one sensory impression you might use. _____

   _____

22.1 Understanding Essays

The Parts of an Essay

An essay is a longer composition in which all parts focus on one main point.

MAIN PARTS OF AN ESSAY	
Title	Attracts attention and gives an indication of the main point and the tone
Introduction	Presents the main point in a thesis statement
Body	Presents subtopics of the thesis statement
Conclusion	Wraps up the essay with a reminder of the thesis statement

Unity and Coherence in Essays

An essay must have unity and coherence both within each paragraph and throughout the essay as a whole.

EXERCISE A: Understanding an Essay. Read the essay below. Then answer the questions that follow it.

(1) The English language experienced great expansion as the British Empire itself expanded territorially. Wherever English explorers established new colonies, they also had to acquire new words for the plants, animals, features, and customs they found there. The great voyages of the English explorers of the sixteenth and seventeenth centuries added a large number of words to our language.

(2) Early voyages to the East and Africa led explorers to add or adapt words for such natural phenomena as *typhoon* and *monsoon*. Also from the East come *tea, bungalow, kimono, dungarees, tycoon,* and *sheik*. From Africa explorers brought back the words *safari, gumbo, yam,* and *banana*.

(3) Later, explorers to the New World encountered a wide range of unfamiliar plants, wildlife, dwellings, and clothing for which no words existed in English. These explorers began to use or adapt the Native American words and took the words back to their homeland as well. From this experience we now have such words as *tobacco, squash, pecan, succotash, raccoon, skunk, moose, toboggan, moccasin, wampum, tipi, wigwam, papoose,* and many others.

(4) Other European explorers made similar additions of words to their languages as a result of their experiences. Many of these have been taken into English too, but less directly. As explorations and colonization have made America a melting pot, these same factors have made English a "melting-pot language."

1. Which sentence is the thesis statement? _____

2. What two subtopics support the thesis statement? _____

3. What kind of support is used to develop the two subtopics? _____

4. What is the writer's general purpose? _____

5. What would be a good title for the essay? _____

EXERCISE B: Recognizing Overall Unity and Coherence. Use the essay above to answer these questions.

1. What is the order of the two body paragraphs? _____

2. What transitions are used? _____

3. What is one main word that is repeated throughout? _____

4. Which sentence in the conclusion is a reminder of the thesis statement? _____

5. What other information does the conclusion give? _____

22.2 Writing an Essay

Prewriting

1. Write a suitable topic on the line below. Make sure it's narrow enough.

TOPIC: _____

2. Now write your audience, making one up if necessary.

AUDIENCE: _____

3. Next write the main point you want to make in your essay.

MAIN POINT: _____

4. Now state your purpose.

PURPOSE: _____

5. Next write your thesis statement. Try out a few before writing one below.

THESIS STATEMENT: _____

6. On a separate piece of paper, brainstorm for support. What does your audience need to know? The answers are your support.

7. Look at your page of support. Identify major subtopics.

SUBTOPICS: _____

8. Choose an order for your subtopics, group your supporting information by subtopic, and eliminate any unnecessary information.

ORDER: _____

9. Outline the body of your essay, again on a separate piece of paper.

10. Jot down ideas for the title, introduction, and conclusion.

Writing

Use your outline to write a complete first draft on a separate piece of paper. Use transitions and other linking devices, and keep your audience in mind as you write. Remember this is just a first draft.

Revising

Write *yes* or *no* to each of the following questions. Then rework your first draft to fix all the items marked *no*.

1. Does the title attract attention, suit the essay, and suggest the main point? _____

2. Does the introduction capture the reader's interest, provide necessary background information, establish the tone, and lead to the thesis statement? _____

3. Does the thesis statement present a clearly focused main point? _____

4. Does each body paragraph develop a subtopic with enough support? _____

5. Are the subtopics closely related to the thesis statement? _____

6. Are the subtopics in a logical order? _____

7. Does each paragraph in the body have a clear topic sentence? _____

8. Does the support in each paragraph follow a logical order? _____

9. Have you used appropriate transitions and other linking devices from paragraph to paragraph? _____

10. Does the conclusion recall the thesis statement and bring the essay to a satisfactory end? _____

After you have improved your paragraph by turning the *no's* into *yes's*, **proofread** carefully, looking for errors in grammar, mechanics, and spelling. If necessary, make a final copy and **proofread** it again.

22.3 Writing Different Kinds of Essays

Writing Expository Essays

The purpose of an expository essay is to present information. Concentrate on explaining your main point to a particular audience.

SAMPLE THESIS STATEMENTS FOR EXPOSITORY ESSAYS
Young adult novels offer realistic situations often combined with a high level of humor and human insight. When the United States purchased Alaska in 1867, few people realized the many future rewards it held.

Writing Persuasive Essays

The purpose of a persuasive essay is to convince the reader to accept an idea or to act. Concentrate on persuading an unsympathetic reader to accept your view.

SAMPLE THESIS STATEMENTS FOR PERSUASIVE ESSAYS
If the Olympics are to continue as a major world event, a number of changes must be made over the next decade. Despite the arguments of critics, the spirit of nationalism is a key part of the success of the modern Olympics.

EXERCISE A: Planning an Expository Essay. Circle one of the topics below. Then complete the prewriting activities that follow it.

Consumer protection and the law   The proliferation of bumper stickers
Plants and herbs for medicine   Prime-time television offerings
"The best things in life are free"   The value of manners

1. Identify your audience. _____

2. Write a thesis statement. _____

   _____

3. List your subtopics. _____

4. Tell what order you would use for the subtopics. _____

5. List one term that you would define. _____

EXERCISE B: Planning a Persuasive Essay. Circle one of the topics below. Then complete the prewriting activities that follow it.

Educating children at home   Unmarked police cars
Censorship in school libraries   Human organ donations
Christmas commercialism   Honesty in job interviews

1. Will you argue for or against the topic? _____

2. Will your audience agree with you or not? _____

3. Write your thesis statement. _____

   _____

4. List your subtopics. _____

5. List one argument from the other side that you will counter in your essay. _____

   _____

23.1 Understanding Research Papers

Sources of Information

A research paper should give credit to its sources in the footnotes at the bottom of the page or at the end of the paper. A research paper should also contain a bibliography that lists all sources consulted.

Sample Footnote	Sample Bibliographical Entry
[1]Anne Edwards, Matriarch (New York: William Morrow, 1984), p. 324.	Edwards, Anne. Matriarch. New York: William Morrow, 1984.

Structures and Features

In addition to citations and a bibliography, discussed above, a research paper has the same general structure and features as an essay.

FEATURES OF A RESEARCH PAPER	
Title	Prepares the reader for the topic
Introduction	Prepares the reader, focuses the topic, and presents a thesis statement
Body	Develops the thesis statement through logical presentation of supporting subtopics
Conclusion	Ties together the thesis statement and the supporting evidence

EXERCISE A: Using Sources of Information. Circle one of the topics below. Use the library card catalog and *The Readers' Guide* to find five sources on your topic. Write a footnote and a bibliographical entry for each source.

The treasures of Tutankhamen   The cost of college
Jai alai   April Fool's Day
Davy Crockett   Anne Boleyn

Footnotes   *Bibliographical Entries*

1. _____   6. _____

_____   _____

2. _____   7. _____

_____   _____

3. _____   8. _____

_____   _____

4. _____   9. _____

_____   _____

5. _____   10. _____

_____   _____

EXERCISE B: Understanding the Structure of a Research Paper. Answer each of the following questions about a research paper.

1. How long is a normal introduction? _____

2. Where is the thesis statement usually found? _____

3. In what part of a research paper are subtopics usually developed? _____

4. What should relate ideas and guide a reader through a research paper? _____

5. What elements of the paper should the conclusion tie together? _____

_____

23.2 Writing a Research Paper

Prewriting

1. Select a topic that is interesting, that can be supported with enough information, and that is narrow enough for a report. Write it below.

TOPIC: _____

2. On a separate piece of paper, write three to five questions you plan to answer through research.
3. On the same paper, write a rough draft of your thesis statement.
4. On note cards, list complete information about each source you plan to use.
5. On note cards, take accurate notes to answer the questions you asked about your topic. Remember to include page references on each card.
6. When your finish your research, make final decisions about your audience and purpose. Then revise your thesis statement to reflect your research.

AUDIENCE: _____

PURPOSE: _____

THESIS STATEMENT: _____

7. Choose the subtopics that your paper will cover.

SUBTOPICS: _____

8. Organize your note cards according to subtopics.
9. Decide what organization—chronological, spatial, order of importance, or developmental—you will use.

ORDER: _____

10. On separate paper, prepare a formal outline of the body of your paper.
11. On the same paper, jot down ideas for a title, introduction, and conclusion.

Writing

Use your outline and notes to write a complete first draft on separate paper. Don't aim for perfection in all details, since this is just a first draft. Do, however, add citations carefully as you write.

Revising

Write *yes* or *no* to each of the following questions. Then rework your first draft to fix all the items marked *no*.

1. Does the introduction arouse interest, give necessary background information, and include the thesis statement? _____

2. Does the thesis statement present a clear main point? _____

3. Does the body present subtopics that develop the thesis statement? _____

4. Are the body paragraphs arranged in a logical order? _____

5. Does each body paragraph have a topic sentence? _____

6. Are the ideas in each paragraph arranged logically? _____

7. Are transitions used with and between paragraphs? _____

8. Does the conclusion contain a reminder of the thesis statement that summarizes the main point of the paper without sounding repetitious? _____

9. Are all quotations and nonoriginal facts and ideas cited in the text of the paper or in footnotes? Are all sources listed correctly in the bibliography? _____

After you have improved your report by turning the *no's* into *yes's*, **proofread** carefully, looking for errors in grammar, mechanics, and spelling. If necessary, make a final copy and proofread it again.

24.1 Book Reports

Understanding Book Reports

A book report presents information about a work and makes a recommendation.

PARTS OF A BOOK REPORT	
Introduction	Identifies the book by title and author and gives a brief summary of the contents
Body	Focuses on specific elements of the book, such as theme, character, or setting
Conclusion	Gives an overall evaluation of the book and makes a recommendation

EXERCISE A: Understanding a Book Report. Carefully read the book report below. Then complete the questions that follow.

(1) *A Separate Peace*, by John Knowles, is a very moving novel about a teenage boy's struggle to find inner peace. It centers on the relationship between Gene, the main character, and his best friend,   /
Phineas. From his interactions with Phineas, Gene learns a great deal about himself and is eventually forced to come to terms with aspects of his personality that he finds quite distasteful.

(2) The story takes place at the Devon School, a small boys' preparatory school in New England. Gene returns to the school as an adult, and his reflections about his experiences there as a student during the 1950's form the main action of the novel.

(3) Phineas is a very interesting and unique character. He is different from the other boys at the school, but he is extremely popular. He is an exceptional athlete and dares to dress in an unusual manner. However, he has problems academically and is somewhat less self-assured than he appears to be on the surface.

(4) Through excellent use of characterization, John Knowles grips the reader's emotions. *A Separate Peace* is a beautifully written novel that is worthwhile reading for both adolescents and adults.

1. What is the setting of the novel? _____

2. Who are the two major characters? _____

3. What are two qualities that make Phineas an interesting character? _____

4. What is the writer's overall evaluation of the novel? _____

5. What is the writer's evaluation based on? _____

EXERCISE B: More Work with Book Reports. Answer the following questions concerning the book report above.

1. What information is presented in the introduction? _____

2. What element of the novel is discussed in the second paragraph? _____

3. What element of the novel is discussed in the third paragraph? _____

4. List two important elements that are not discussed. _____

5. What information is presented in the conclusion? _____

24.1 Writing a Book Report

Prewriting

1. Select a book that you have read recently.

| TITLE: | _____ | AUTHOR: | _____ |

2. Choose two elements of the book to discuss.

ELEMENTS: _____

3. Gather and list supporting information for both elements.

SUPPORTING INFORMATION: _____ _____

_____ _____

_____ _____

_____ _____

4. Choose an order for the elements you are going to discuss.

ORDER: _____

5. Decide what information you are going to present in your introduction.

INTRODUCTION INFORMATION: _____

6. Decide what kind of evaluation you want to give in the conclusion.

EVALUATION: _____

7. On separate paper, use your list of support and other notes to outline your report.

Writing

Use your outline to write a complete first draft on a separate piece of paper. As you are writing, refer to your list of supporting ideas and concentrate on connecting your ideas with transitions. Remember that this is just a first draft and that it does not have to be perfect.

Revising

Write *yes* or *no* to each of the following questions. Then rework your first draft to fix all the items marked *no.*

1. Is the book clearly identified by title and author in the introduction? _____

2. Does the introduction give an overview of the book? _____

3. Do the elements discussed represent the book accurately? _____

4. Have you given enough supporting information to make your ideas clear to the reader? _____

5. Have you chosen the best support available in the book? _____

6. Is all the information relevant? _____

7. Have you used quotation marks correctly and given page numbers following any direct quotations from the book? _____

8. Does your conclusion make a definite recommendation to the reader? _____

9. Have you used transitions and other linking devices to make your ideas flow smoothly? _____

After you have improved your book report by turning the *no's* into *yes's,* **proofread** carefully, looking for errors in grammar, mechanics, and spelling. If necessary, make a final copy and **proofread** it again.

24.2 Papers Analyzing Literature

Understanding Literary Analysis Papers

A literary analysis paper helps interpret a work for readers. Like an essay, a literary analysis paper focuses on a main point, supported by evidence taken from the work.

PARTS OF A LITERARY ANALYSIS PAPER	
Title	Names the work being analyzed and or indicates the main point of the paper
Introduction	Identifies the work and author, specifies the kind of work, and states the main point that will be made in the paper
Body	Presents subtopics of the main point and supports the main point with quotations, examples, and details
Conclusion	Recalls the main point in the introduction and pulls the paper together as a whole

EXERCISE A: Understanding a Literary Analysis Paper. Carefully read the paper below. Then answer the questions that follow.

The Central Symbol in "Birches"

(1) In Robert Frost's poem "Birches," a young boy swinging through the air on tree branches is the central symbol of the poem. The boy's swinging represents a unity between human beings and nature, as well as the human desire to find a temporary escape from reality.

(2) The narrator speaks of the unity that exists between the boy and the birch trees that take the place of other children as his companions in play. The boy lived "too far from town to learn baseball." (Line 25) So, instead of developing special relationships with other children, the boy develops a sense of oneness with the birch trees on his father's land. He learns all there is "To learn about not launching out too soon; And so not carrying the tree away; Clear to the ground." (Lines 33–35)

(3) The idea of being able to swing out into the air and land safely on the ground symbolizes the notion of a temporary escape from reality. The narrator speaks of the need to find such an escape when "life is too much like a pathless wood." (Line 44) Expressing this desire to find temporary relief from his daily existence, the narrator points out how wonderful it is to be able to climb up the tree toward heaven only to be gently set back down to the earth. He states that it is "good both going and coming back." (Line 59)

(4) So, as the central symbol of the poem, the image of a boy swinging on birches can be understood on two different levels. It not only points out the union that can exist between a person and nature but also expresses the human desire to find temporary refuge from reality.

1. What is the main point stated in the introduction? _____
2. How does the title help prepare the reader for the main point? _____
3. What other information is presented in the introduction? _____
4. What subtopic is discussed in the second paragraph? _____
5. What subtopic is presented in the third paragraph? _____

EXERCISE B: More Work with Literary Analysis. Answer the following questions concerning the paper above.

1. How is the first subtopic related to the main idea? _____
2. How is the second subtopic related to the main idea? _____
3. Give an example of supporting information presented under the first subtopic. _____
4. Give an example of supporting information presented under the second subtopic. _____
5. Which sentence in the conclusion refers back to the main topic? _____

W
R
I
T
I
N
G

P
R
O
C
E
S
S

P
A
G
E

24.2 Writing a Literary Analysis Paper

Prewriting

1. Choose a work that you have read recently in literature class or on your own.

TITLE: _____ **AUTHOR:** _____

2. Choose one element to discuss in your paper.

ELEMENT: _____

3. Write three questions dealing with the element you have chosen to help you analyze the work.

ANALYSIS QUESTIONS: _____

_____

4. Answer these questions.

ANSWERS: _____

5. Using the answers to your analysis questions, make a rough list of supporting information.

SUPPORTING INFORMATION: _____

_____

6. Use your list of information to decide what the main point of your paper will be.

MAIN POINT: _____

7. Decide on three subtopics.

SUBTOPICS: _____

_____

8. On separate paper, make a general plan for your paper.

9. Use your list of supporting information to prepare an outline on a separate sheet of paper.

Writing

Use your outline to write a first draft on a separate sheet of paper.

Revising

Write *yes* or *no* to each of the following questions. Then rework your first draft to fix all the items marked *no.*

1. Does the title of the paper reflect your main point? _____

2. Is the main point clearly stated in the introduction? _____

3. Does the body of the paper develop the main point with supporting information organized in subtopics? _____

4. Is there enough support to develop the main point fully? _____

5. Is all the information directly relevant to the main point? _____

6. Are any direct quotations from the work complete and accurate? _____ Are page (or line) numbers given? _____

7. Does the conclusion recall the main point made in the introduction? _____

8. Are all paragraphs and subtopics clearly connected? _____

9. Are all the sentences smooth and clear? _____

After you have improved your paragraph by turning the *no's* into *yes's,* **proofread** carefully, looking for errors in grammar, mechanics, and spelling. If necessary, make a final copy and **proofread** it again.

25.1 Journals

Understanding Journals

A journal is a personal record of events, feelings, observations, or special interests.

KINDS OF JOURNALS	
Purposes of Journals	**Probable Writing Time**
To keep track of everyday events	Daily
To express candid feelings and insights	Daily or several times a week
To record key events or moments in life	Weekly
To record experiences in an area of special interest	As each occasion arises

Keeping a Journal

Use vivid, significant details as you record events and thoughts in chronological order.

EXERCISE A: Understanding the Purpose of Journal Entries. Read each item below and determine the purpose of the journal the writer is keeping.

EXAMPLE: Meeting my first niece was a thrilling experience.   *To record key events*

1. Yesterday's problems with Jed have been forgotten, and today our relationship is back to normal.

   _____

2. I wish I could learn to stay calm in a crisis. _____

3. The part of the trip that I enjoyed the most was our visit to Buckingham Palace. _____

4. During today's Explorer's hike I found an interesting rock. _____

5. Today Joy finally told me the secret she has been holding back. _____

EXERCISE B: Planning a Journal Entry. Choose one of the topics below or a topic of your own. Then answer the questions to plan a journal entry.

      The first day of a vacation   Your reactions to an unexpected success
      Overcoming an obstacle   A problem with getting along with someone
      Making a difficult decision   Saying goodbye to someone you care for

1. When? _____

2. Who? _____

3. Where? _____

4. What? _____

   _____

   _____

5. Your reactions: _____

   _____

25.2 Writing a First-Person Narrative

Prewriting

1. Identify a specific person, place, or thing to write about.

TOPIC: _____

2. Choose two incidents involving this person, place, or thing to focus in on.

INCIDENTS: _____

_____

_____

3. Write four questions concerning your topic that will help you to brainstorm for information.

QUESTIONS: _____

_____

_____

_____

4. Answer these questions to compose a list of information.

INFORMATION: _____

_____

_____

_____

5. Arrange this information in chronological order.

ORDER: _____

_____

6. Think of some descriptive details that will enliven your composition for your readers.

DESCRIPTIVE DETAILS: _____

_____

_____

Writing

Use your lists of information and descriptive details to draft your narrative. As you write, keep in mind the key features of a first-person narrative and concentrate on maintaining a clear chronological presentation. Remember that this is only a first draft and that you will have an opportunity to improve it.

Revising

Write *yes* or *no* to answer each of the following questions. Then rework your first draft to fix all the items marked *no*.

1. Does your narrative stick to its subject without straying onto tangents? _____

2. Are events presented in clear chronological order, with a logical beginning and end? _____

3. Have you included enough descriptive details to keep the reader interested? _____

4. Have you included personal observations that will help the reader understand your feelings about the subject? _____

5. Is a first-person point of view maintained throughout? _____

After you have improved your paragraph by turning the *no's* into *yes's*, **proofread** carefully, looking for errors in grammar, mechanics, and spelling. If necessary, make a final copy and **proofread** it again.

25.2 Writing an Autobiography

Prewriting

1. Write the time span that your autobiography will cover.

TIME SPAN: _____

2. Identify the setting.

SETTING: _____

3. Next, list the incidents you want to include.

INCIDENTS: _____

_____

4. Next, identify the characters you want to include.

CHARACTERS: _____

_____

5. Arrange the incidents into the order in which you will present them.

ORDER: _____

_____

6. Select some descriptive details about the setting you have chosen that will help you to visualize what you are writing about.

DETAILS: _____

_____

7. Select some descriptive details about the characters you have chosen.

DETAILS: _____

_____

Writing

Use the plans you have sketched above to write a first draft of your autobiography. Concentrate on presenting events and details from a consistent first-person point of view to give the reader a clear idea of what was happening and how you felt about it. Remember that this is only a first draft and that you will have an opportunity to improve it.

Revising

Write *yes* or *no* to answer each of the following questions. Then rework your first draft to fix all the items marked *no*.

1. Have you consistently presented your material from a first-person point of view? _____

2. Are the time span and the setting identified for the reader? _____

3. Have you followed clear chronological order? _____

4. Have you included enough vivid details and dialogue to make people and places come alive for the reader? _____

5. Have you included your personal feelings and insights about the incidents you present? _____

After you have improved your paragraph by turning the *no's* into *yes's,* **proofread** carefully, looking for errors in grammar, mechanics, and spelling. If necessary, make a final copy and **proofread** it again.

26.1 Understanding Short Stories

Character and Plot

A character in a short story creates one dominant impression. The plot of a short story is a series of events growing out of a conflict.

STAGES OF A PLOT	
Exposition	Introduces the setting and major characters; establishes the narrator's point of view; gives necessary background information
Opening Incident	Creates a conflict and gets the plot going
Rising Action	Presents further incidents or insights that intensify the conflict
Climax	Raises the conflict to its highest point; changes the course of events
Falling Action (not always used)	Relaxes the conflict to prepare readers for the conclusion
Conclusion	Resolves the conflict and brings the plot to an end

Point of View

A story is narrated from a single, consistent point of view.

KINDS OF NARRATORS	
First Person	The narrator tells the story as he or she saw it and usually participates in the action.
Limited Third Person	The narrator is outside of the story and cannot see into the characters' minds.
Omniscient Third Person	The narrator is outside of the story but is able to see into the characters' minds.

Dialogue

Dialogue helps to create believable characters and to develop the plot.

EXERCISE A: Recognizing the Stages of a Plot. Identify each item below as (1) exposition, (2) opening incident, (3) rising action, (4) climax, (5) falling action, or (6) conclusion.

EXAMPLE: After the rescue, reporters crowded around the two boys. __5__

1. The pair exchanged a hearty handshake, glad that the ordeal was over. _____

2. The boys set out never dreaming of the adventure that lay before them. _____

3. Joe stopped beside a dark mine shaft. "Hey, Ken," he said, "let's take a look inside." _____

4. With Ken's first step into the old mine, the earth slipped away beneath his feet. _____

5. When the sliding debris and crashing beams had settled, the boys screamed for help. _____

EXERCISE B: Identifying Kinds of Narrators. Identify the point of view expressed in each item below as (1) first person, (2) limited third person, or (3) omniscient third person.

EXAMPLE: Pete's head was pounding and his stomach was churning. __3__

1. I heard the wind whistling about outside and realized that it would be a cold day. _____

2. Harriet and Frank moved slowly through the crowd. _____

3. Bill smiled confidently, though he could feel tension building inside his stomach. _____

4. All day I remained troubled by the startling news I had overheard. _____

5. Paula tapped her fingers impatiently and wondered, "What can they be up to?" _____

26.2 Writing a Short Story

Prewriting

1. Decide on the main character of your story.

MAIN CHARACTER: _____

2. Write down key details about this character: name, age, sex, appearance, personality traits, and manner of speech.

CHARACTER DETAILS: _____

_____

3. List the other major characters that you will include in your story.

MAJOR CHARACTERS: _____

_____

4. Decide what kind of conflict your main character will become involved in. Then state your conflict in a single sentence.

CONFLICT: _____

5. Write down some details of the setting, including time and place.

SETTING: _____

6. Keeping in mind the kind of conflict you will have, decide on the type of narrator you will use.

POINT OF VIEW: _____

7. Prepare a plot outline based on character and conflict.

EXPOSITION: _____

OPENING INCIDENT: _____

RISING ACTION: _____

CLIMAX: _____

FALLING ACTION: _____

CONCLUSION: _____

Writing

Follow your plot outline to write a first draft of your story maintaining a consistent point of view. Concentrate on connecting the events using transitions and on making the dialogue fit your characters and situations. Remember that this is only a first draft and that you will have a chance to improve it.

Revising

Write *yes* or *no* to answer each of the following questions. Then rework your first draft to fix all the items marked *no.*

1. Is the point of view clear and consistent? _____

2. Does the plot develop in a logical way, with an exposition, rising action, climax, and conclusion? _____

3. Is the conflict, whether internal or external, made clear to the reader? _____

4. Does the dialogue accurately reflect the way people in such a position would actually talk? _____

After you have improved your paragraph by turning the *no's* into *yes's,* **proofread** carefully, looking for errors in grammar, mechanics, and spelling. If necessary, make a final copy and **proofread** it again.

27.1 Looking at Letters

Friendly Letters and Social Notes

The five basic parts of a friendly letter and social note are the heading, the salutation, the body, the closing, and the signature. Use either either indented or semiblock style.

Heading	Your address and the date
Salutation	The greeting (Dear _____,)
Body	Any information you want to send
Closing	A slightly formal, casual, or affectionate sign-off
Signature	Your name

Business Letters

A business letter contains a heading, an inside address, a salutation, a body, a closing, and a signature. Use either block, modified block, or semiblock style.

SPECIAL RULES FOR BUSINESS LETTERS
Write on unlined, 8½ × 11 inch white paper with a matching envelope.
Type your business letter, if possible.
Double space between paragraphs and between other parts of the letter.
Leave a margin of one inch on all sides of the paper.

EXERCISE A: Working with the Parts of Friendly Letters. Follow the instructions below.

1. Write two headings, the first in indented style and the second in semiblock style.

_____   _____
_____   _____
_____   _____

2. Write two salutations.

_____   _____

3. Write two closings and signatures, the first in indented style and the second in semiblock style.

_____   _____
_____   _____

4. Which parts of a friendly letter begin on the right? _____

5. Which parts begin on the left? _____

EXERCISE B: Working with the Parts of a Business Letter. Follow the instructions below.

1. Write two inside addresses.

_____   _____
_____   _____

2. Write two salutations.

_____   _____

3. In which style does everything begin on the left? _____

4. What should go on the top of the second page? _____

5. What should you do before sending out a business letter? _____

27.2 Writing Letters

Writing Friendly Letters and Social Notes

Friendly letters should include well-organized statements of personal information. Social notes should focus on a specific purpose.

KINDS OF SOCIAL NOTES	
Type	**Purpose**
Invitation	To invite people to a social event
Letter of Acceptance	To accept an invitation
Letter of Regret	To explain your inability to attend
Thank-you Note	To express gratitude
Letter of Congratulations	To recognize another's achievement
Letter of Condolence	To express sympathy

Writing Business Letters

Write business letters that are clear and direct.

KINDS OF BUSINESS LETTERS	
Type	**Purpose**
Request	To request information or material
Order	To place an order for something
Application	To apply for a position
Complaint	To request the correction of a mistake
Opinion	To express an opinion

EXERCISE A: Planning a Friendly Letter. Complete the following prewriting activities.

1. Write the name of someone you could send a personal letter to. _____

2. List some interests or shared experiences that you and this person have in common. _____
_____

3. List one piece of information or one idea you could tell this person about. _____
_____

4. List one recent event that you could tell this person about. _____
_____

5. List any questions you could ask this person. _____
_____

EXERCISE B: Planning a Business Letter. Choose one type of business letter described in the chart above. Then complete the prewriting activities below.

1. What is the purpose of your business letter? _____

2. Who is the audience for your letter? _____

3. What essential information should be included? _____
_____

4. List specific information (that you make up) in the order in which you would write it in the letter.
_____

5. Write the first sentence of your letter. _____

28.1 Preparing Answers to Essay Exams

Planning Your Time

Plan your time before you begin an essay exam and check to make sure you remain on schedule.

Interpreting the Question

Look for word clues and other indications that show what kind of information you should supply.

Clues	What You Should Do
resemblances, similarities	Look for similarities.
contrast, differ	Look for and stress differences.
define, explain	Tell what something means or is.
describe	Give the main features with examples.
diagram, draw, chart	Give a drawing or a chart.
discuss, explain	Make a general statement and support it.
explain, why, what, how	Give information that tells why, what, or how.
illustrate, show	Give concrete examples and explain them.
interpret, significance	Explain certain statements or events.
in your opinion	Support a position with facts and reasons.
If . . . then, What . . . if	Support a prediction with facts and reasons.

EXERCISE A: Interpreting Essay Exam Questions. For each question below, underline the key word or words. Then tell what you should do to answer it.

EXAMPLE: <u>Discuss</u> the role of religion in the conflict in the Middle East. *Make a general statement and support it.*

1. What are the similarities between today's music and the music of the fifties? _____
   _____

2. Chart the developing role of women in the work force over the past fifty years. _____
   _____

3. In your opinion, what man or woman has had the greatest impact on American society in the
   twentieth century? _____

4. How does rugby differ from American football? _____

5. Discuss the advances made in the area of medicine in the past fifty years. _____
   _____

EXERCISE B: More Work with Essay Exam Questions. Follow the directions in Exercise A.

1. Write a brief paragraph defining romanticism. _____

2. Describe the setting of *A Separate Peace* by John Knowles. _____

3. What were the reasons for American involvement in the Vietnam War? _____
   _____

4. What will the world be like if scientists are successful in developing laser weapons for use in outer
   space? _____

5. What is the significance of Kino's inability to sell his pearl for an appropriate price in *The Pearl* by
   John Steinbeck? _____

28.1 Preparing Answers to Essay Exams

Planning and Writing Your Answer

Organize supporting information in a modified outline and then write your answer.

Checking Your Answer

Proofread your answer for clarity and correctness.

CHECKING YOUR ANSWER
Does at least one sentence present the main answer to the question?
Does the answer directly answer the question that was asked?
Is the topic sentence or thesis statement clear?
Does all of the support clearly relate to the main point of the answer?
Is there enough support to fully answer the question?
Is the supporting information well organized?
Do transitions connect the ideas?
Does the answer end persuasively with a concluding idea?
Are all the words, including any corrections, readable?
Are there any grammatical, mechanical, or spelling errors?

EXERCISE A: Planning an Answer to an Essay Question. Choose one of the following essay exam questions. Then answer the questions below.

> Compare and contrast two famous authors.
> Discuss the role of computers in education.
> How has American football changed over the past fifty years?
> What would happen if children were not required to attend school?
> Define rock music.

1. Make a list of ideas that seem to answer the question. _____

   _____

2. Write a single statement that sums up your ideas. _____

   _____

3. List your ideas in a logical order. _____

   _____

4. Add a concluding idea to your outline. _____

   _____

EXERCISE B: Writing and Proofreading an Answer to an Essay Exam Question. Use the answers you wrote in Exercise A to write a paragraph-length answer to the essay question you chose on a separate piece of paper. Proofread your answer.

29.1 Increasing Your Vocabulary

Making Good Use of Resource Material

Use the dictionary and special vocabulary sections of your notebook regularly to build your vocabulary. Use a thesaurus to find a list of words similar in meaning.

Dictionary	Thesaurus
Spelling: mol-li-fy Pronunciation: (mäl'əfī') Meaning: pacify; appease	Words similar in meaning: *mollify:* calm, relieve, soften

Recognizing Related Words

Synonyms are words similar in meaning; antonyms are words opposite in meaning; homonyms sound alike but have different meanings and spellings.

Synonyms	Antonymns	Homonyms
hate/dislike	good/evil	one/won

EXERCISE A: Using a Dictionary and a Thesaurus to Increase Vocabulary. Use a dictionary to look up the definition of each word below, and write the definition in the space provided. Then use a thesaurus to find a synonym for each word.

EXAMPLE: momentous | *very important* | *eventful*

Word	Definition	Synonym
1. monotonous	_____	_____
2. finesse	_____	_____
3. scandalous	_____	_____
4. testimony	_____	_____
5. declaim	_____	_____
6. furbish	_____	_____
7. admonish	_____	_____
8. dulcify	_____	_____
9. curtail	_____	_____
10. zealous	_____	_____

EXERCISE B: Recognizing Related Words. Identify each set of words as synonyms, antonyms, or homonyms.

EXAMPLE: bass-base _____*homonyms*_____

1. characterize/describe _____
2. militarist/pacifist _____
3. meter/metre _____
4. sanity/foolishness _____
5. initiate/begin _____
6. raze/raise _____
7. midget/dwarf _____
8. cycle/circuit _____
9. advantage/impediment _____
10. flew/flue _____

29.1 Increasing Your Vocabulary

Remembering Vocabulary Words

Use one or more review techniques to remember the meaning of new words.

STUDYING AND REVIEWING METHODS
1. Set up an individual three-column vocabulary notebook. 2. Use index cards to make a set of flashcards. 3. Work with a tape recorder. 4. Study with a partner.

EXERCISE A: Keeping a Vocabulary Notebook. Look up the meaning of each of the following words. Then write a bridge word and a definition for each one.

EXAMPLE: dastardly ___*dud*___ ___*mean and cowardly*___

1. deacon _____ _____
2. holograph _____ _____
3. kirk _____ _____
4. bey _____ _____
5. cowl _____ _____
6. languid _____ _____
7. revile _____ _____
8. salvo _____ _____
9. wadi _____ _____
10. maw _____ _____

EXERCISE B: Using Other Study Methods. Use a dictionary to look up the definition of each word below, and write the definition in the space provided. Copy each word on one side of an index card. On the other side, copy its definition. Work with a partner, quizzing each other on the definitions.

EXAMPLE: hypocrite ___*a person who pretends to be what he is not*___

Word	Definition
1. paradigm	_____
2. escapade	_____
3. nihilism	_____
4. enunciate	_____
5. buoyancy	_____
6. amorphous	_____
7. tantamount	_____
8. tantalize	_____
9. repulse	_____
10. haughty	_____

29.2 Using Context

Recognizing Context Clues

Use context clues to determine the meanings of unfamiliar words.

USING CONTEXT CLUES
1. Read the sentence without the unknown word.
2. Look for clues in the surrounding words.
3. Make a guess.
4. Try your guess in the sentence.
5. Check your guess in the dictionary.

Using Context Clues in Daily Reading

Use context clues to determine the meaning of unfamiliar words you come across in your everyday reading.

Using Context Clues in Textbook Reading

Use context clues to determine the meaning of unfamiliar words in textbook reading.

Using Context Clues in Other Kinds of Reading

Use context clues to determine the meaning of unfamiliar words in your reading for research.

EXERCISE A: Using Context Clues. Read the following paragraph. Make guesses about the underlined words and write your guesses in the spaces below. Then check the meanings in a dictionary and change your guesses where necessary.

Taking good photographs is not a matter of investing in an expensive camera and all its (1) accoutrements. Special equipment is (2) indisputably needed for certain shots, but most good pictures are based more on an appreciation of artistic, or (3) aesthetic, qualities and human interest than on huge (4) outlays of cash and (5) cumbersome equipment. Think about the total picture you are taking. Is there any way you can (6) enhance the colors? Adding something red can often greatly improve a scene taken outdoors. Is there any way you can (7) encapsulate the picture, perhaps by adding a border of leaves at the top or side? Above all, consider your center of interest. Don't try to get too many things into each picture. Find the most (8) intriguing aspect of a general scene and focus on that. Cut out all the (9) extraneous things going on around this part of the scene. Capture the one thing that most interests you and your (10) prospective viewers.

EXAMPLE: investing _____putting money into_____

1. accoutrements _____
2. indisputably _____
3. aesthetic _____
4. outlays _____
5. cumbersome _____

6. enhance _____
7. encapsulate _____
8. intriguing _____
9. extraneous _____
10. prospective _____

EXERCISE B: Using Words in Context. Choose five of the words in Exercise A and use them in sentences of your own. Try to help the reader by providing context clues.

EXAMPLE: _____Harold is thinking about investing his savings in a new company._____

1. _____
2. _____
3. _____
4. _____
5. _____

29.3 Using Structure

Using Prefixes

Use the meanings of prefixes to determine the meanings of unfamiliar words.

TEN COMMON PREFIXES			
ab-	away	post-	after
circum-	around	pre-	before
com- (co-, col-		re-	back
con-, cor-)	together	semi-	half
ex- (e-, ec-, ef-)	from	sub- (suc-,	
inter-	between	suf-, sup-)	under

EXERCISE A: Finding Words with Common Prefixes. Use a dictionary to find a word beginning with each prefix. Then define each word in a way that helps illustrate the meaning of the prefix. Use any of the spellings shown in the chart.

EXAMPLE: com-   _contain_   _hold together_

1. ab-   _____   _____

2. circum-   _____   _____

3. com-   _____   _____

4. ex-   _____   _____

5. inter-   _____   _____

6. post-   _____   _____

7. pre-   _____   _____

8. re-   _____   _____

9. semi-   _____   _____

10. sub-   _____   _____

EXERCISE B: Using Prefixes to Determine Meaning. Make a guess about the meaning of each of the following words. Then look up your guesses in a dictionary and make any necessary changes.

EXAMPLE: predestined   _already known although in the future_

1. abscission _____

2. circumspect _____

3. connote _____

4. exude _____

5. interstellar _____

6. postnatal _____

7. preliterate _____

8. repatriate _____

9. semidetached _____

10. substratum _____

29.3 Using Structure

Using Roots

Use roots to determine the meanings of unfamiliar words.

TEN COMMON ROOTS			
-ced- (-ceed-, -cess-)	go	-puls- (-pel-)	drive
-dic- (-dict-)	say	-spec- (-spect-)	see
-graph-	write	-ten- (-tain-, -tin-)	hold
-mit- (-mis-)	send	-ven- (-vent-)	come
-pon- (-pos-)	put	-vert- (-vers-)	turn

Using Suffixes

Use suffixes to determine the meanings and parts of speech of unfamiliar words.

NINE COMMON SUFFIXES			
Suffix	**Meaning**	**Example**	**Part of Speech**
-able	capable of	reliable	adjective
-ance	the act of	clearance	noun
-ate	to make	decorate	verb
-fy	to make	clarify	verb
-ist	a person who	violinist	noun
-ize	to make	idolize	verb
-less	without	careless	adjective
-ous	marked by	pompous	adjective
-tion	state of being	action	noun

EXERCISE A: Using Roots to Determine Meaning. Make a guess about the meaning of each of the following words. Then look up your guesses in a dictionary and make any necessary changes.

EXAMPLE: retain   _to hold back_

1. recession _____

2. abdication _____

3. stenographer _____

4. remission _____

5. deposition _____

6. compulsion _____

7. circumspect _____

8. sustain _____

9. intervene _____

10. diversion _____

EXERCISE B: Using Suffixes to Help Determine Meaning. Circle the words that offer the better definition for each word.

EXAMPLE: solidify   (become hard)   with difficulty

1. witless   beyond hope   without intelligence

2. duplication   identical copy   extremely puzzled

3. animate   bring to life   striped horse

4. aerialist   add space   high-wire acrobat

5. tortuous   extremely crooked   cause pain

29.4 Exploring Etymologies

Borrowed Words

Loanwords are words in the English language that have been borrowed from other languages.

BORROWED WORDS		
Latin—tabulate	French—pallet	Spanish—alpaca
Greek—autocracy	Dutch—sputter	Italian—squadron

Words with New Meanings

The English language grows by giving new meanings to old words. Additionally, many new words are added to the language when two existing words are joined together to form a third word with a new meaning.

WORDS WITH NEW MEANING	
houseboat	typewriter
switchboard	stockbroker

Coined Words

The English language also grows through the addition of newly coined words.

EXERCISE A: Finding the Sources of Words. Look up these words in a dictionary that provides etymologies and write the language of origin.

EXAMPLE: relate _____Latin_____

1. splice _____
2. reiterate _____
3. squall _____
4. calligraphy _____
5. platitude _____

6. taboo _____
7. rejoin _____
8. collate _____
9. agency _____
10. operetta _____

EXERCISE B: Combining Words to Create New Words. Combine a word from the following list with each numbered word to form a new word.

water	cycle	keeper	dumb	cow
wood	pole	shirt	road	trade

EXAMPLE: _____watermark_____

1. mark _____
2. bell _____
3. tail _____
4. motor _____
5. flag _____

6. goal _____
7. block _____
8. shed _____
9. hide _____
10. color _____

30.1 Improving Your Spelling

Proofreading Carefully

Proofread everything you write for spelling errors. Use a dictionary to look up words that you suspect may be spelled incorrectly.

Studying Spelling Demons

Review a list of spelling demons to identify words that you may have trouble spelling correctly.

STEPS FOR MASTERING SPELLING DEMONS
1. Try each demon in a sentence of your own.
2. Check to see if you have spelled it correctly.
3. Add any misspelled demons to your personal spelling list.

EXERCISE A: Proofreading a Selection. There are ten misspelled words in the paragraph below. Find them and spell each word correctly in the spaces after the paragraph.

The food in the school cafateria is usually inedable. Sometimes I wonder if I will contract food poisening from eating the green hambergers or the brown tuna salad. I'm sure that some of the fod is left out for days before being surved. None of the leftovers are ever trown out either. Last week, they served fried chicken one day and Italian sauseges the next day. Then they combined the two to make chicken with spicey Italian sause the next day.

1. _____   6. _____

2. _____   7. _____

3. _____   8. _____

4. _____   9. _____

5. _____   10. _____

EXERCISE B: Mastering Spelling Demons. Complete each of the following sentences, filling in the missing letters in each spelling demon.

EXAMPLE: She finished the seventh report and began the ei___*ghth*___.

1. We plan to eat in a new Italian re_____ tonight.

2. Jody did well in science but failed ma_____ .

3. The se_____ typed twenty-three letters yesterday.

4. The so_____ class is planning a party.

5. The thunder roared and li_____ filled the sky.

6. Asparagus is just one of the ve_____ I hate.

7. Jeff decided to join the French Fo_____ Legion.

8. This Fe_____ I am not sending any Valentines.

9. The Morgans are celebrating their fiftieth wedding an_____ .

10. Mark that date on your ca_____ .

30.1 Improving Your Spelling

Keeping a Spelling Notebook

Make a personal spelling list of difficult words, enter it in your notebook, and keep it up to date.

SPELLING LIST FORMAT			
Misspelled Words	Correct Spelling	Practice Sessions	Memory Aids
~~apparent~~ ~~criticise~~	apparent criticize	✓ ✓	the appa<u>rent</u> <u>rent</u> criti<u>ci</u>ze and ama<u>ze</u>

Studying Problem Words

Study the words in your personal spelling list using the steps in the following chart.

STEPS FOR STUDYING PROBLEM WORDS
1. Look: Study all letters in the word carefully. 2. Pronounce: Say the word out loud. 3. Write: Put the word on paper. 4. Check: See if you have written the word correctly. 5. Review: Repeat the steps until you know each word.

Developing Memory Aids

Use memory aids to remember the spelling of words that you find especially difficult.

METHODS FOR DEVELOPING MEMORY AIDS
1. Find a word within the word: the appa<u>rent</u> <u>rent</u>. 2. Find a word with the same letters: criti<u>ci</u>ze and ama<u>ze</u>.

EXERCISE A: Studying Problem Words. Look at each of the following words and underline the letter or letters that are likely to cause problems.

EXAMPLE: condem<u>n</u>

1. sophomore	6. misspell	11. courtesy	16. vacancy
2. absence	7. desperate	12. calendar	17. pretense
3. omitted	8. creditor	13. privilege	18. ninety
4. eighth	9. mysterious	14. parallel	19. concede
5. scissors	10. correspondence	15. occurrence	20. truly

EXERCISE B: Creating Memory Aids. Create a short memory aid for each word.

EXAMPLE: similar   simil<u>ar</u> l<u>ar</u>ks

1. familiar _____	6. conscience _____
2. rehearse _____	7. category _____
3. dessert _____	8. permissible _____
4. license _____	9. surprise _____
5. laboratory _____	10. bulletin _____

30.2 Following Spelling Rules

Plurals

The plural form of most nouns is formed by adding *-s* or *-es* to the singular. The forms of other nouns are listed in the dictionary.

SAMPLE PLURALS			
Singular	**Plural**	**Singular**	**Plural**
miss	misses	goose	geese
mix	mixes	mother-in-law	mothers-in-law
fizz	fizzes	mouse	mice
wish	wishes	phenomenon	phenomena
puppy	puppies	woman	women
tomato	tomatoes	radio	radios
daisy	daisies	fire engine	fire engines

EXERCISE A: Writing Plurals. Write the plural of each word in the space provided.

EXAMPLE: leash ___*leashes*___

1. child _____
2. poppy _____
3. lace _____
4. rhythm _____
5. bench _____
6. fox _____
7. deer _____
8. mouse _____
9. potato _____
10. flash _____

11. sister-in-law _____
12. radius _____
13. fuss _____
14. station wagon _____
15. piano _____
16. goose _____
17. boy _____
18. watch _____
19. bird _____
20. moose _____

EXERCISE B: More Work with Plurals. In each blank, fill in the correct plural form of the word in parentheses.

EXAMPLE: Six ___*witnesses*___ saw the crime being committed.   (witness)

1. Fallen _____ were scattered across the ground.   (leaf)
2. The _____ raced to the scene of the crime.   (police car)
3. Ten rock _____ performed at the festival.   (group)
4. All of the _____ in the kitchen are dull.   (knife)
5. Most of the _____ at the convention were boring.   (speech)
6. He had a team of _____ pulling his cart.   (ox)
7. The _____ were crying all night.   (baby)
8. Several _____ were unable to attend the meeting.   (man)
9. Two of Joey's _____ were knocked out when his brother hit him in the face.   (tooth)
10. Lois and Alice were the _____ of their departments.   (editor-in-chief)

30.2 Following Spelling Rules

Prefixes and Suffixes

When a prefix is added to a word, the spelling of the root word remains the same. The spelling of the prefix, however, may change. When a suffix is added to a word, the spelling of the root word may change. Check a dictionary when in doubt.

ADDING PREFIXES	
With No Change	**With Prefix Change**
com + motion = commotion dis + locate = dislocate in + coherent = incoherent sub + basement = subbasement	com + respond = correspond dis + fuse = diffuse in + legal = illegal sub + press = suppress

ADDING SUFFIXES	
With No Change	**With Change**
enjoy + able = enjoyable rely + ing = relying separate + ly = separately anger + ed = angered	day + ly = daily rely + able = reliable separate + ing = separating omit + ed = omitted

EXERCISE A: Adding Prefixes. Combine the following items, using a dictionary when necessary.

EXAMPLE: in + migrate _immigrate_

1. dis + appear _____
2. in + luminate _____
3. sub + marine _____
4. com + mend _____
5. mis + spell _____
6. dis + own _____
7. in + legitimate _____
8. com + pare _____
9. co + ordinate _____
10. sub + ordinate _____
11. un + favorable _____
12. dis + solve _____
13. com + rode _____
14. mis + giving _____
15. in + numerable _____
16. sub + pose _____
17. mis + use _____
18. in + migrate _____
19. dis + fer _____
20. com + rect _____

EXERCISE B: Adding Suffixes. Combine the following items.

EXAMPLE: promote + ed _promoted_

1. brag + ing _____
2. state + ment _____
3. create + ing _____
4. differ + ence _____
5. delay + ed _____
6. decrease + ing _____
7. innocent + ly _____
8. snap + er _____
9. cry + ing _____
10. wonderful + ly _____
11. try + ed _____
12. occur + ing _____
13. engage + ed _____
14. love + ly _____
15. replay + able _____
16. deny + ed _____
17. encourage + ment _____
18. annoy + ed _____
19. usual + ly _____
20. employ + ment _____

30.2 Following Spelling Rules

ie and ei Words

Use the traditional rule for *ie* and *ei* words after you have learned the exceptions.

ie Exceptions		*ei* Exceptions		
ancient	financier	either	height	seize
conscience	science	foreign	leisure	sheik
efficient	sufficient	forfeit	neither	weird

Words Ending in -cede, -ceed, and -sede

Memorize the spellings of words that end in *-cede*, *-ceed*, and *-sede*.

Words Ending in -cede		Words Ending in -ceed	Word Ending in -sede
accede	precede	exceed	supersede
concede	recede	proceed	
intercede	secede	succeed	

EXERCISE A: Spelling ie and ei Words. Add *ie* or *ei* to complete each sentence.

EXAMPLE: After today, Keith will _e_ _i_ ther quit or be fired.

1. How many cards have we rec___ ___ved so far?

2. The ch___ ___f reason for the new policy is to avoid overcrowding.

3. If the team isn't here soon, they will forf___ ___t the game.

4. Cannons put an end to the long s___ ___ges.

5. Mr. Thorn considered the s___ ___zure of his goods an outrage.

6. Who painted this c___ ___ling purple?

7. Ms. Eldon firmly bel___ ___ved in miracles.

8. The next customer spoke with a for___ ___gn accent.

9. Mrs. Carry found an ingenious way to spend her l___ ___sure time.

10. We were not dec___ ___ved by his pleasant smile.

EXERCISE B: Spelling Words Ending in -cede, -ceed, and -sede. Fill in the correct letters in the spaces below.

EXAMPLE: The candidate would not con__*cede*__, even though it was clear that he had been defeated.

1. The principal was forced to inter_____ when a fight broke out in the cafeteria.

2. The president's orders super_____ those of the general manager.

3. You must pro_____ with extreme caution.

4. To suc_____ in life you must set high standards for yourself.

5. When Joe looked in the mirror he discovered that his hairline had started to re_____ .

6. The mechanic told me that the cost of the repairs would ex_____ his original estimate.

7. I must con_____ that point to you.

8. After arguing for several hours, I finally realized that I would have to ac_____ to the mechanic's demands.

9. John's band will pre_____ the main act in tonight's concert.

10. After losing the election, the candidate decided to se_____ from the Republican Party.

30.2 Following Spelling Rules

Other Confusing Endings

Learn to distinguish between similar word endings that may cause spelling errors.

Words Ending in *-ance*		Words Ending in *-ence*	
appearance	importance	absence	independence
brilliance	reluctance	correspondence	presence
elegance	tolerance	difference	violence

THREE CONFUSING PAIRS	
The Common Ending	**The Less Common Ending**
-ary: dignitary, library	-ery: bakery, cemetery, winery
-cy: diplomacy, policy	-sy: courtesy, ecstasy, fantasy
-ify: dignify, qualify	-efy: liquefy, putrefy, stupefy

EXERCISE A: Adding Confusing Endings. Add one of the endings in the charts above to complete each sentence. Use a dictionary when necessary.

EXAMPLE: We were shocked at her abs___*ence*___ from the ceremony.

1. Ursula Le Guin's stories often deal with fanta_____.

2. What does a runner have to do to qual_____?

3. All of their correspond_____ begins that way.

4. Her hesitan_____ was not expected.

5. You would be foolish to place any reli_____ on the machine.

6. Two bodyguards appeared with each foreign dignit_____.

7. What is the signific_____ of this latest bulletin?

8. His performance on this tennis court is legend_____.

9. Sitting on the counter, the meat is likely to putr_____.

10. Those movies absolutely terr_____ me.

EXERCISE B: More Work with Confusing Endings. Follow the directions in Exercise A.

1. Ellen bought two dozen cookies at the bak_____.

2. The teacher told Nate's parents that he had superior intellig_____.

3. He is certainly not a viol_____ man.

4. Sometimes Betty's actions stup_____me.

5. Some people consider frog's legs to be a delica_____.

6. Elena recently accepted a position with an advertising agen_____.

7. When Joe could not get into college, he decided to join the milit_____.

8. When the army refused to accept him, Joe entered a monast_____.

9. After Joe had moved into his new retreat, he discovered that he had epilep_____.

10. Once he learned to cope with his condition, Joe moved to New York and got a job at a nurs_____.

31.1 Good Study Habits

Developing a Study Plan

Develop a Study Plan in order to manage your time most efficiently. Your study plan should include setting up a study area, establishing a study schedule, and using an assignment book.

MAKING A STUDY SCHEDULE
1. Block out areas of time in which you have activities. 2. Block out study periods of no longer than forty-five minutes each. 3. Schedule study periods for times when you are most alert. 4. Arrange to study your most difficult subjects first. 5. Make use of study hall and free time at school to get some assignments completed.

Setting Goals

Set long- and short-term goals to improve your study habits. Record these goals and your timetable for achieving them in writing.

SETTING LONG- AND SHORT-TERM GOALS		
Long-term Goal: To develop a study plan		
Short-term Goals	**Timetable**	**Comments**
To set up a study area	1 week (by March 5)	Successfully completed
To establish a study schedule	2 weeks (by March 12)	Successfully completed
To use an assignment book to keep track of long- and short-term assignments	1 month (by March 29)	Still need to learn to divide long-term assignments into short-term goals

EXERCISE A: Setting Up a Study Schedule. Use the spaces provided below to make up a study schedule that suits your personal needs. Be sure to include at least two hours of study time.

Time	Activity
8:00–3:00	School
_____	_____
_____	_____
_____	_____
_____	_____
_____	_____

EXERCISE B: Setting Goals for Study Skills. Select one study skill that you want to master. Then complete the steps below.

1. Set a long-term goal. _____
2. Set a short-term goal. _____
3. Set a second short-term goal. _____
4. Set a third short-term goal. _____
5. Now set a timetable for your short-term goals. _____

Copyright © by Prentice-Hall, Inc.

31.2 Methods of Taking Notes

Making Outlines

Use a modified outline to take notes while listening or reading. Use a formal outline to arrange ideas when preparing major written and oral assignments.

Modified Outline	Formal Outline

Grizzly Bears
—Native to western North America
—Very large animals
—Omnivorous
—Coats vary from light brown
    to almost black
	I. Grizzly Bears
	  A. Native to western North America
	    1. Idaho, Montana, Wyoming
	    2. Alaska, western Canada
	  B. Very large animals
	    1. Up to 8 feet long
	    2. Weight up to 800 pounds
	  C. Omnivorous
	  D. Coats vary from light brown to
	      almost black

Writing Summaries

Use a summary to take notes when you need to remember only the main ideas.

Summary
Grizzly bears are very large, omnivorous animals that are native to western North America.

EXERCISE A: Making a Modified Outline. Listen to a radio or TV interview or a segment of a documentary. Or listen to a recording of a speech. Use the questions below to prepare a modified outline of what you hear.

1. Who is the source of the information? _____

2. When and where was the information presented? _____

3. What is the main idea? _____

4. What are the supporting ideas? _____

_____

_____

5. On a separate piece of paper, write the main idea and supporting ideas in modified outline form.

EXERCISE B: Writing a Summary. Read a newspaper or magazine article. Use the questions below to plan a summary of your article.

1. What is the title of the article and who wrote it? _____

2. Where and when was it published? _____

3. What was the main idea of the article? _____

4. What are the supporting ideas? _____

_____

_____

5. On a separate piece of paper, write the main idea and supporting ideas in summary form.

32.1 Forms of Reasoning

Using Fact and Opinion

Analyze material first to decide whether it is reliable.

DISTINGUISHING BETWEEN FACT AND OPINION	
Statements of Fact	Objective statements that can be verified
Statements of Opinion	Subjective statements that cannot be verified but must be supported with related facts before being accepted as valid

Using Valid Reasoning

Think logically to draw valid conclusions.

FORMS OF REASONING		
Form	**Valid Use**	**Invalid Use**
Inference	A reasonable interpretation of the information that is given	An interpretation that is not consistent with the given information
Generalization	A statement that holds true in a large number of cases or is supported by evidence	A statement that is made without accounting for exceptions
Analogy	A comparison between two different objects or events that are similar in some important way	A comparison that fails to account for essential dissimilarities
Cause and Effect	A sequence in which something is caused by one or more events that occurred before it	A sequence in which the first event did not cause the second event

EXERCISE A: Distinguishing Between Facts and Opinions. Identify each of the following statements as a *fact* or *opinion*.

EXAMPLE: Dwight Gooden is the best pitcher of all time. ___*opinion*___

1. John Updike is a better writer than Harold Robbins. _____

2. Mt. Washington is the tallest mountain in New England. _____

3. The New York Yankees have won the World Series more times than any other
   team. _____

4. The average man is larger than the average woman. _____

5. Women are smarter than men. _____

EXERCISE B: Analyzing Forms of Reasoning. Identify the form of reasoning in each of the following statements as *inference, generalization, analogy,* or *cause and effect.* Then, for each case, tell whether the conclusion drawn is valid or invalid.

EXAMPLE: Dogs do not get along with cats. ___*generalization*___ ___*invalid*___

1. An infant's brain is like an empty canvas. _____ _____

2. Wendy writes very well, has an excellent understanding of grammar, and reads with a high
   comprehension level, so she should do well in English class. _____

   _____

3. Football players are not good students. _____ _____

4. Because of the icy roads, there were many car accidents last night.

   _____ _____

5. Human beings are like snowflakes—no two people are exactly alike.

   _____ _____

32.2 Language and Thinking

Uses of Language
Learn to identify different uses of language.

USES OF LANGUAGE	
Denotation and Connotation	The *denotation* of a word is its literal or exact meaning. The *connotation* of a word is its suggested or implied meaning.
Self-Important Language	*Self-important language* consists of scholarly, technical, or scientific words and overly long phrases.
Slanting	*Slanting* refers to the fact that writers and speakers select and arrange words to communicate the meaning they want to convey.

EXERCISE A: Analyzing the Uses of Language. Identify each of the items below as being an example of *denotation, connotation, self-important language,* or *slanting.*

EXAMPLE: In an attempt to formulate an intelligible visualization of our future possibilities, we are prioritizing our options. *self-important language*

1. Mr. Jones is suffering from a severe dysfunction of his left cerebral hemisphere.

_____

2. The man walked slowly down the street. _____

3. The woman crawled at a snail's pace down the busy street as if she had no place to go.

_____

4. The fact that its students have a tendency to do poorly on standardized tests proves that Webster High School is an inferior school. _____

5. This politician is a truly evil man, who cares for no one other than himself.

_____

EXERCISE B: More Work with the Uses of Language. Follow the directions in Exercise A.

1. The fact that the air quality in Boston and Buffalo is better than it was five years age makes it quite clear that pollution is no longer a problem in this country. _____

2. Randy strutted through the crowd as if he thought he was the king of the world.

_____

3. As is the case in any military engagement, our ultimate objective is the total pacification of our enemies. _____

4. The home team won the game. _____

5. For the first time in the school's history, a student has been expelled for cheating on a test. Today's students are not as honest as students from past years.

Reading Skills

Reading Textbooks

Use reading and study aids in your textbooks to help you understand what you are reading and to remember it better later.

USING THE SQ4R METHOD	
Survey	Preview the material you are going to read.
Question	Turn each heading into a question.
Read	Answer the questions you have posed.
Recite	Orally recall the questions and answers.
Record	Take notes to further reinforce information.
Review	Review the material on a regular basis.

Varying Your Reading Style

Change your reading style whenever your purpose in reading changes.

DIFFERENT READING STYLES		
Style	**Definition**	**Use**
Phrase Reading	Reading groups of words in order to understand all material	For studying, solving problems, and following directions
Skimming	Skipping words in order to read rapidly and get a quick overview	For previewing, reviewing, and locating information
Scanning	Reading in order to locate a particular piece of information	For research, reviewing, and finding information

EXERCISE A: Using the SQ4R Method. Choose a chapter in one of your textbooks to use in completing the work below.

1. List the chapter headings and subtitles. _____

_____

2. Turn two of these headings into questions. _____

_____

3. Read the chapter. Then answer the questions you wrote in #2. _____

_____

4. List the main ideas contained in the chapter. _____

_____

5. List the major details used to support one of these ideas. _____

_____

EXERCISE B: Varying Your Reading Style. Skim through a chapter in one of your textbooks and write a summary. Then read through the chapter again using the phrase reading method and write a modified outline.

33.1 Reading and Test-Taking Skills

Reading Critically

Read critically in order to question, analyze, and evaluate what you read.

CRITICAL-READING SKILLS
1. The ability to distinguish between fact and opinion
2. The ability to identify the author's purpose·
3. The ability to make inferences
4. The ability to recognize the author's tone
5. The ability to recognize persuasive techniques

EXERCISE A: Identifying Author's Purpose. Read each of the items below and determine whether the author's purpose is *to inform, to instruct, to offer an opinion, to sell,* or *to entertain.*

EXAMPLE: The first step in learning how to maintain your own car is gaining an understanding of how the engine works. ___*to instruct*___

1. In 1974 Henry Aaron hit his 715th home run, breaking Babe Ruth's record for most home runs in a major league career. _____

2. In a recent taste test, people preferred our cola to the leading brand by a ratio of three to one. _____

3. After examining statistics regarding alcohol-related traffic fatalities, it should be quite clear to anyone that the penalties for driving while intoxicated should be much stiffer. _____

4. Do you ever get tired of being bombarded by commercials? Do you ever get tired of listening to people try to convince you that the quality of your life would be greatly improved if you switched laundry detergents? _____

5. To carve a turn, you must drive your knees into the hill, with your weight on your downhill ski. _____

EXERCISE B: Recognizing Author's Tone. Identify the author's tone in each item below as *positive, neutral,* or *negative.*

EXAMPLE: Last night the candidate gave an extremely inspiring speech about tax reform. ___*positive*___

1. Sources close to the President indicate that it is unlikely that he will sign the bill. _____

2. To say that the officiating in last night's game was horrendous would be an understatement. _____

3. In their final concert of the season, the band performed flawlessly, giving what was perhaps their finest performance ever. _____

4. There was general agreement among those of us who had taken time out of our busy schedules to listen to the speech that the candidate's words were without substance. _____

5. In his nationally televised address last night, the President urged the American people to support him in his efforts to reach an arms control agreement with the Soviet Union. _____

33.2 Test-Taking Skills

Taking Objective Tests

Budget your time among previewing the test, answering the questions, and proofreading.

OBJECTIVE TEST-TAKING STRATEGIES	
Previewing	Skim through the test and figure out how much time you will give to each set of questions.
Answering	Go with your first response to a question unless you have good reason to change it.
Proofreading	Make sure that you have followed directions completely and answered all the questions.

Mastering Different Kinds of Objective Questions

Learn specific strategies for handling objective questions to achieve higher test scores.

MASTERING DIFFERENT KINDS OF OBJECTIVE QUESTIONS	
Multiple Choice	Try to answer the questions before looking at the possible answers.
Matching	Match easy items first, lightly crossing out each used answer.
True/False	Pay special attention to words that can make the difference between a true or false statement.
Fill-in	Use specific information rather than general statements.

EXERCISE A: Taking a Matching Test. Match the capitals on the right with the countries on the left. Then proofread your answers.

EXAMPLE: Span __k__   k. Madrid

1. Canada _____   a. Montevideo
2. Austria _____   b. Ottawa
3. U.S.S.R. _____   c. Paris
4. France _____   d. Rangoon
5. Ireland _____   e. Vienna
6. Chile _____   f. Santiago
7. Uruguay _____   g. Moscow
8. Liberia _____   h. Berlin
9. East Germany _____   i. Dublin
10. Burma _____   j. Monrovia

EXERCISE B: Taking a True/False Test. Write *true* or *false* to answer each question. Then proofread your answers.

EXAMPLE: There are only three kinds of objective questions. __*false*__

1. Proofreading is not an important part of taking a test. _____
2. A person's first answer will often be correct. _____
3. Matching questions always have the same number of items in both columns. _____
4. Trying to answer a question before looking at the choices can help. _____
5. Unless there is a penalty for guessing, you should answer all questions. _____

33.2 Test-Taking Skills

Taking Standardized Tests

Prepare for standardized tests by completing all your class assignments carefully and reading as much and as widely as you can.

ANSWERING QUESTIONS ON THE PSAT	
Antonym Questions	Look for a word among the answer choices that is as opposite to the given word as possible and is the same part of speech.
Analogy Questions	Define both words in the initial pair and define the relationship between these two words, making sure that you keep the pair of words in the order given.
Sentence Completion Questions	Read the sentence and try to fill in the blanks(s) before looking at the choices. Use signal words to predict the correct answer.
Reading Comprehension Questions	Preview the questions before reading the passage, keeping them in mind when you are reading the passage.

EXERCISE A: Answering Analogy Questions. Choose the pair of words whose relationship is most similar to that expressed by the capitalized pair.

EXAMPLE: CARROT:VEGETABLE:: __B__
(A) dog:mouse   (B) apple:fruit   (C)tree:oak   (D) teacher:frankfurter   (E)car:driver

1. SURGEON:HEART::_____
   (A) student:teacher   (B) razor:beard   (C)cake:baker   (D) dentist:tooth   (E) lunatic:crazy

2. ATHEIST:BELIEVER::_____
) (A) stop:start   (B) miserly:philanthropist   (C) cake:candy   (D) pessimist:optimist   (E) win:lose

3. LIZARD:SNAKE::_____
   (A) bird:parrot   (B) dog:hydrant   (C) beaver:platypus   (D) fudge:chocolate   (E) frog:amphibian

4. EXPEDITE:FACILITATE::_____
   (A) exculpate:exile   (B) pliability:pleasantry   (C) try:win   (D) confuse:complicate
   (E) keep:rectify

5. SHOE:LACE::_____
   (A) sleeve:shirt   (B) engine:automobile   (C) meat:gravy   (D) cat:tail   (E) guitar:string

EXERCISE B: Answering Sentence Completion Questions. Choose the word that best completes the meaning of each sentence.

EXAMPLE: His feet _____ because his shoes were too tight. __A__
         (A) ached   (B) sweat   (C) itched   (D) uncomfortable   (E) big

1. Billy had to _____ before the end of the concert.
   (A) leave   (B) stop   (C) dance   (D) choose   (E) cruise

2. As a result of her _____, Gilda had to stay after school.
   (A) teeth   (B) voice   (C) tardiness   (D) test   (E) teacher

3. Jack saw an _____ crawling up his leg.
   (A) slug   (B) apple   (C) snake   (D) ant   (E) elephant

4. The mayor accused his aide of _____ funds.
   (A) misappropriating   (B) using   (C) eating   (D) dishonesty   (E) relieving

5. After his sister's death, Joe _____ for weeks.
   (A) crying   (B) lamented   (C) mortified   (D) pontificated   (E) stopped

34.1 Using the Library

Knowing What You Are Looking For

Begin your research by knowing basic facts about your topic: correct spelling, alternate names, and time period.

Using the Card Catalog

Use word-by-word alphabetizing to find a title, author, subject, analytic, or cross-reference card for the book you need. In addition, recognize the following special filing rules.

Actual Name	Will Be Found Under
The Three Musketeers	*Three Musketeers*
Abigail McKinley	McKinley, Abigail
Mr. Johnson Arrives	*Mister Johnson Arrives*
30 Days in China	*Thirty Days in China*

Going From Catalog to Shelf

Use call numbers and other symbols given on the catalog cards to locate materials on the shelves.

Item	Method of Finding on the Shelf
Nonfiction	Use a call number.
Fiction	Find the fiction section and then look for the author's last name.
Biography	Find the biography section and then look for the subject's last name.
Reference Book	Find the reference section and then use the call number.

EXERCISE A: Using the Card Catalog. Follow the instructions below.

1. Write the first three letters you would look under to find these names.

   a. Charles Dickens _____   c. Phyllis McGinley _____

   b. *The Last Day* _____   d. *Dr. Jekyll and Mr. Hyde* _____

2. Put the following in card catalog order, using 1 for the first card and 6 for the last.

   a. *East Lynn* _____   c. *East of Eden* _____   e. *East Meets West* _____

   b. *Eastern Religions* _____   d. *Easter Plays* _____   f. Eastman, Max _____

3. Give two alternate names you would look under if you found no card listed for MONARCHS, ENGLISH.

   a. _____   b. _____

EXERCISE B: Finding Books on the Shelves. Write the first three letters or numbers you would look for to find each of the following books.

EXAMPLE: *So Big* by Edna Ferber (fiction)   *FER*

1. *Aeronautics* by Andrew Coles (683.72C) _____

2. *Emily Dickinson* by Drew Phillips (biography) _____

3. *Dombey and Son* by Charles Dickens (fiction) _____

4. *The Civil War Revisited* by Anne Herrold (973.21H) _____

5. *Enrico Caruso* by Phyllis Charles (biography) _____

34.2 Using Reference Materials

General Reference Books

Use general reference books to check basic facts or to explore the range of a topic.

General Reference Books	What They Contain
Encyclopedias	Basic informaton about almost all general topics
Almanacs	Facts and statistics on a wide range of subjects, including sports, governments, and famous people
Atlases	Current or historical maps, often showing more than just political or geographic details
Gazetteers	Facts about places around the world

Specialized Reference Books

For detailed information about a limited aspect of a broad topic, consider specialized dictionaries (such as *Webster's Dictionary of Synonyms*), specialized encyclopedias (such as the *Encyclopedia of World Art*), biographical reference books (such as *Current Biography*), and literary reference books (such as *Bartlett's Familiar Quotations*).

Periodicals and Pamphlets

Use magazines, newspapers, and pamphlets to supplement your research with specialized or current information. Learn to use *The Readers' Guide to Periodical Literature* to find magazine articles quickly.

Readers' Guide Entry	What It Means
An early habitat of life. D. Groves. Sci Am 245:64–74 O '81	An article entitled "An Early Habitat of Life" by D. Groves in *Scientific American,* Volume 245, Pages 64–74, October 1981 issue

EXERCISE A: Finding Reference Materials. For each of the following, list the title of the reference work in your school library that you would go to first.

EXAMPLE: The population of Chicago ___*Information Please Almanac*___

1. A short biography of Al Pacino _____
2. Three major cities in Poland _____
3. The names of top professional golfers _____
4. A word that means "delicious" _____
5. A short biography of Queen Victoria _____

EXERCISE B: Using *The Readers' Guide*. Read the following entry and then give the details requested below.

> Apocalypse in the Alps. J. Murphy.
> Time 124:66 S 3 '84

1. Date of magazine _____
2. Name of magazine _____
3. Page on which article appears _____
4. Name of article _____
5. Name of author _____

34.3 Using the Dictionary

Recognizing Kinds of General Dictionaries

Use a dictionary that suits your present academic needs. When choosing a dictionary, look up several words to make sure the dictionary is neither too hard nor too easy.

Finding the Words

Become familiar with the spelling patterns of the sounds in English words.

STEPS FOR FINDING WORDS QUICKLY
1. Use the four-section approach. (A-D, E-L, M-R, S-Z)   2. Next, use the guide words.   3. Then follow strict alphabetical order.

Knowing What Dictionaries Contain

Learn to recognize and use the various features of your own dictionary.

Features	Ways in Which They Can Be Used
Front matter	To learn more about the specific dictionary you have
Spelling	For revising your papers
Syllabification	For breaking words at the ends of lines
Pronunciation	For any speaking situations
Part-of-Speech Labels	To check for correct usage
Inflected Forms (Plurals, etc.)	To find the correct form
Etymologies (Histories of Words)	To help remember meanings
Definitions	To understand what you are reading
Usage Labels (Slang, etc.)	To find the right tone for your writing
Field Labels (Elec., etc.)	To find technical meanings
Idioms (Head Off, etc.)	To understand special phrases
Derived Words (With Suffixes)	To find the correct form and spelling
Synonyms	To find alternate words

EXERCISE A: Recognizing the Many Uses of a Dictionary. Answer the following questions.

1. What three features of the dictionary do you use most often?

    a. _____

    b. _____

    c. _____

2. What are two other features that you can benefit from using when you are writing and revising your papers?

    a. _____

    b. _____

EXERCISE B: Using Your Dictionary. Use your dictionary to answer the following.

1. What is one technical meaning of *lead*? _____

2. What is one idiom listed under *jump*? _____

3. Which syllable is stressed in *paternal*? _____

4. What part of speech is *megrim*? _____

5. What is the plural of *focus*? _____

35.1 Group Discussions

Recognizing Different Kinds of Group Discussions

A group discussion is formed to achieve a specific common goal.

KINDS OF GROUP DISCUSSIONS	
Committees	A small group of a larger organization formed to discuss specific ideas
Round-table Discussion Groups	Groups formed in order to share information
Panels	A group of several informed people who hold a discussion with an audience present
Symposiums	A group in which each member gives a formal speech dealing with one aspect of a topic with an audience present

Planning a Group Discussion

A group discussion should focus on a topic that is timely and interesting and which the members are involved with and prepared to discuss.

PLANNING A GROUP DISCUSSION
1. Determine the discussion topic.
2. Define the topic precisely.
3. Make an outline of points to be discussed.
4. Research the topic.

Participating in a Group Discussion

Active participation is required of all members for an effective group discussion.

EXERCISE A: Recognizing Different Kinds of Group Discussions. Identify the kinds of group discussions referred to in each item below.

EXAMPLE: A group of executives discuss how to meet a deadline. ___*committee*___

1. A lawyer, a doctor, a scientist, and a book editor speak to a group of college students about potential careers. _____

2. A group of students discuss extracurricular activities at their school. _____

3. Members of a law firm discuss how to present a case. _____

4. Several politicians discuss relevant issues before a group of citizens from a small town.

   _____

5. Five professional athletes speak about violence in their respective sports before a group of fans.

   _____

EXERCISE B: Planning a Group Discussion. Complete the activities below.

1. Choose a topic. _____

2. Define the topic precisely. _____

3. Phrase the topic as a question. _____

   _____

4. On a separate sheet of paper, make an outline of points to be discussed.

5. List two sources that you will use in researching the topic. _____

   _____

35.2 Parliamentary Procedure

Basic Principles of Parliamentary Procedure

Parliamentary procedure guarantees that the rights of the majority and the minority are respected and that a meeting is conducted in an orderly way.

```
PRINCIPLES OF PARLIAMENTARY PROCEDURE

  1. Issues are debated and voted on one at a time.
  2. The decision of the majority rules.
  3. Those in the minority are allowed to present their views.
  4. Every member has a right to vote or not to vote.
  5. Open discussion of every issue is assured.
```

Holding a Meeting

Parliamentary procedure regulates the way the business of a meeting is conducted and the duties of the chairperson.

```
STEPS FOR CONDUCTING A MEETING

  1. Call to order
  2. Roll call
  3. Reading and approval of minutes from last meetings
  4. Reading of reports of officers
  5. Reading of reports of committees
  6. Consideration of old (unfinished) business
  7. Consideration of new business
  8. Adjournment
```

EXERCISE A: Understanding Parliamentary Procedure. Answer the questions below.

1. When and where was parliamentary procedure developed? _____

2. What does a simple majority consist of? _____

3. How are minority rights protected? _____

4. Does every member have to speak at each meeting? _____

5. What is the voting percentage needed to limit or end debate? _____

EXERCISE B: More Work with Parliamentary Procedure. Answer the questions below.

1. What is the list of steps for conducting a meeting called? _____

2. Is it necessary for the chairperson to remain neutral during a discussion? _____

3. Is the chairperson allowed to vote? _____

4. What is a motion? _____

5. List four of the steps involved in carrying out a motion. _____

_____

_____

_____

_____

35.3 Public Speaking

Recognizing Different Kinds of Speeches

Choose the kind of speech you will give by considering both the purpose of the speech and your audience.

KINDS OF SPEECHES	
Expository	Given to explain an idea, a process, or an object
Persuasive	Given to try to get the listeners to agree with the speaker's position or to take some action
Entertaining	Given to offer the listeners something to enjoy

Giving a Speech

Follow a series of steps to plan, prepare, practice, and deliver your speech.

DELIVERING A SPEECH
1. Establish eye contact with several people in the audience.
2. Briefly look over your note cards before you start speaking.
3. Refer to your note cards as seldom as possible once you have started.

Evaluating a Speech

Evaluate a speech in a way that offers benefits to the speaker and to yourself.

EXERCISE A: Planning a Speech. Complete the activities below.

1. Choose the kind of speech you will give. _____

2. Choose an appropriate topic. _____

_____

3. Gather the information you need to give your speech, taking notes on separate paper.

4. On a separate sheet of paper, write an outline that presents the information you gathered in question 3 in a logical manner.

5. Next, prepare note cards that you can use when you deliver your speech.

EXERCISE B: Evaluating a Speech. Evaluate a speech given in class by answering the questions below.

1. What type of speech was given? _____

2. Did the speaker introduce the topic clearly and develop it well? Support your answer. _____

_____

3. Did the speaker support main ideas with appropriate details? Give two examples. _____

_____

4. Did the speaker's movements confirm or contradict his or her words. Where? How? _____

_____

5. Did the speaker vary the pitch of his or her voice? _____

35.4 Listening Skills

Listening for Important Information

Learn to take mental notes of main ideas and major details as you listen.

LISTENING FOR MAIN IDEAS
1. Listen carefully to the beginning statements of the speaker. 2. Visualize the main ideas and repeat them in your own words. 3. Decide whether the speaker's examples, definitions, facts, and statistics support the main ideas you have in mind.

Following Directions

Learn to listen to directions by performing certain mental steps.

Listening Critically

Listen critically in order to interpret and evaluate a speaker's words.

TECHNIQUES FOR LISTENING CRITICALLY	
Fact and Opinion	Be aware of opinions that are disguised as facts.
Denotation and Connotation	Watch for the use of the connotation of a word to distort the truth.
Euphemisms	Be aware that euphemisms are used by speakers to avoid speaking directly about something.
Self-important Language	Watch for the use of self-inflated language to present ideas that could be easily understood if they were stated more clearly and simply.

EXERCISE A: Listening for Important Information. Work on improving your listening skills by writing down the main idea and major details of a lecture given in one of your classes.

1. Main idea _____

2. Major detail _____

3. Major detail _____

4. Major detail _____

5. Major detail _____

EXERCISE B: Developing Critical Listening Skills. Listen critically to a political speech on radio or television. Then complete the activities below.

1. What was the topic of the speech? _____

   _____

2. Did the speaker support all of his or her opinions with facts? How? _____

   _____

3. Did the speaker disguise any of his or her opinions as facts? If so, give an example. _____

   _____

4. Did the speaker use euphemisms? If so, give an example. _____

   _____

5. Did the speaker use self-important language? If so, give an example. _____

   _____